P1

DO LESS, GET MORE

DO LESS
GET MORE

**Guilt-free Ways to Make Time for the
Things (and People) That Matter**

SHÁÁ WASMUND

PENGUIN LIFE

AN IMPRINT OF

PENGUIN BOOKS

PENGUIN LIFE

UK | USA | Canada | Ireland | Australia
India | New Zealand | South Africa

Penguin Life is part of the Penguin Random House group of companies
whose addresses can be found at global.penguinrandomhouse.com.

First published by Portfolio 2015
Published by Penguin Life 2016
001

Text copyright © Sháá Wasmund, 2015

Designed by James Alexander at Jade Design
Illustrations by Helen Wakefield

The moral right of the copyright holders has been asserted

Set in Georgia and Helvetica Neue
Printed in Italy by Printer Trento

A CIP catalogue record for this book is available from the British Library

ISBN: 978–0–241–00369–5

CONTENTS

INTRODUCTION

❛ *Sometimes the questions are complicated and the answers are simple.* ❜

I've been known as the queen of multitasking for too long. Whether from a misguided sense of duty to 'do everything', a constant fear of 'losing out' or an innate need to be 'in control', I've tried to juggle more things than any sane person should attempt or want to do. My phone has been like an umbilical cord and email has ruled my life. Mindfulness was remembering to pick up my keys before I left the house.

Sound familiar? Have you ever found yourself checking your emails or texts while having dinner with your family or friends? Do you feel like there aren't enough hours in the day, that you run around getting nowhere fast? Do you wish you could put what really matters first in your life, but struggle to figure out how?

It's so easy to justify why we do the things we do, but when we take a closer look we begin to see and understand the true consequences of our constant 'busyness'. Are we genuinely enjoying our lives, doing what we love and being with the people who matter? Or are we rushing from one task to the next, trying to be all things to all people, and not feeling like we have the time or energy to give anything or anyone the attention they deserve?

The comfort of being busy

Some time ago my world fell apart when my gorgeous, wonderful partner passed away. He wasn't just my partner, he was my beautiful son's dad, and he was an awesome dad. My coping mechanism was to occupy every minute of my time so that I would have none left to think. It helped me survive, but now I realize I let it possess me like an inner demon. I became trapped in a straitjacket of my own making; if my mind wandered I'd just pull the ties tighter with more responsibilities, more emails, projects, people, more, more, more . . .

And then my son said to me, 'Mummy, you're *always* busy.' I looked back at him. It had taken the eyes of a child to show me what was happening. The light bulb went on. It was time for me to make some decisions about what was really important and start filtering out the noise to hear my own voice – and listen to what it was saying.

When I did that, I realized that the successful projects and relationships in my life – the ones I really connected with, the ones I really wanted – all had something in common: they worked because I gave them my attention *at the right moments.*

When I work with entrepreneurs and people starting up their own businesses, I always encourage them to identify the one thing they can do that day that will make the biggest difference. Not the five things or even the three things: the *one* thing.

Most people seem to believe they need to do more, when really they just need to do what matters. To filter out the distractions and focus on the things that make the difference between surviving and thriving, between playing catch-up and being in the lead.

To become world class at this, you have to give yourself a bit of time and space to let go, let the real you unfold. (Reading this book is perfect.) When you are thinking clearly, you can more easily discover what it is you really want, and then you need consciously to prioritize it; to discriminate between the things that help you grow and the things that set you back – or at least keep you standing still.

11

To make this a reality requires honest, deep thinking, and you must follow that with action. We all place limitations on ourselves, often subconsciously, and until you uncover them, face them and free yourself of them, you'll be stuck on life's hamster wheel.

It's time to look your fears and excuses in the face and prepare to jump out of your comfort zone, to start taking control of your life and to forge time for yourself and the things that matter. Your destination is happiness, and you can enjoy every moment of the journey.

Why are you waiting to be truly happy?

According to recent research from the Royal Economic Society, most people's lifetime happiness curve is U-shaped. Our happiness is high in our youth, starts to trail off by the time we are just twenty-five and doesn't pick up again until we retire. Unsurprisingly, this research indicates that our happiest times are when our lives are simplest, and the pressures of expectation from work and family commitments are at their lowest. That leaves forty years in between – the period when we are considered to be in our mental and physical prime, but during which too many of us settle for being 'crazy busy' and just moderately happy. That's scary. Do we really want to defer living life at its best until we retire?

Of course, this book isn't a 'how to find happiness' manual, much though I'd like it to be. Sadly, there is no secret formula that will solve all life's problems. The best we can do is help each other illuminate the dark corners. My aim is to provide a wake-up call to remind you that it's possible to grab your own happiness and show you how to do it. This book *is* about living life to the fullest and not squandering it. It is for anyone who has something to change and the desire to do so. **It's particularly useful for those with short attention spans and tight schedules.** People who want to know *how*, not just why.

I thought about calling this book *How to Get More Out of Life*, but it isn't about 'getting more stuff'. This book is about taking what you already have and making the most of it – and in order to do so you may need to let go of a few things in the process. It's about squeezing every last drop out of life while you have the time to appreciate it. Getting the best from life is about digging down to the core of who you really are, what you really want and what makes you truly happy, then making the changes necessary to focus on *those* things.

It's about reconnecting with the things that make you smile and your heart sing, the pursuits, the people and the work that give you lasting happiness, the dreams that linger unfulfilled, the adventures you've yet to set off on, the businesses you've always wanted to set up, the places you've wished you'd travelled to, the restaurants you've never eaten in, the lives you want to change, the house by the sea, the yoga at dawn, the book that's never been written, the life you imagined. This isn't a fairy tale, and neither is it wishful thinking. Many, if not most, of the things that will create your *best* life are perfectly attainable if you are willing to stop doing what's not important and start prioritizing what is.

You can do anything ... but you can't do everything. At least not at the same time.

Relight your fire

This isn't a book about time management either, but it will help you to prioritize *how* and *where* you invest your time to create a life you love.

I'm not going to suggest you sell everything you own and go backpacking around the world (although if that's your dream, I'm certainly not going to advise against it). What I will teach you are practical ways to create change, now. It's about appreciating the life you already have and making it better. We're renovating here, not rebuilding.

Most of you reading this book already have a pretty decent life – you just might be so caught up in being busy you've forgotten what it looks like. You have a roof over your head, whether you rent or own; you go on holidays; perhaps you have kids and/or a partner; you definitely have friends and colleagues; you have a job or run your own business. Most of all, you have dreams.

This book is about how we resurrect those dreams and bring more of them to life, by spending less time doing the things we are conditioned to believe we *ought* to do and more time doing the things we *love* to do. It's about relighting your fire and discovering your courage. It's about knowing that you can't please all of the people all of the time . . . and that's OK.

ought: used to give advice, indicate duty or correctness; an expected state

There will be tough times, when you're going to have to face up to your own culpability in holding yourself back (we all do it), but there will be plenty of eureka moments, too. Moments when you realize a few simple changes can make a big difference. That getting the best out of life is possible for everyone, not just a select few.

THE PLACES YOU WANT TO GO

THE THINGS THAT MAKE
YOUR HEART SING

THE PEOPLE WHO MAKE YOU SMILE

THE LIVES YOU WANT TO CHANGE

THE BUSINESS YOU'VE
ALWAYS WANTED

THE HOUSE BY THE SEA

THE YOGA AT DAWN

THE BOOK THAT'S NEVER BEEN
WRITTEN

THE LIFE YOU DREAMED OF

You may think that some of the things I suggest are simplistic, but the truth is we overcomplicate our lives enough. By keeping things simple, we give ourselves a chance of actually succeeding.

Don't dismiss ideas because they seem too simple; that's exactly why they will work.

The best lawyers and accountants are the ones who talk to their clients in everyday language, the ones who don't feel the need to impress people with jargon. The same is true here; if I can get you results in fewer than 250 pages, why give you 500? If you can make meaningful change using simple tools, why give you complicated ones?

Small changes can make a BIG difference

Sometimes life gets so complicated it feels like it doesn't even belong to you any more. You crave simplicity but seem like a bystander watching your own life pass by, helpless to intervene. You can't even begin to think of how you could be less busy, whether you have a demanding boss or you're running your own show. You have a desire to make the most of your skills and your passions. You want to stop running round in circles and instead focus on getting the stuff that's important done, but you just have so much to do, you can't find the time.

However, when you begin to make even the smallest of changes, you start to reclaim your power

to prioritize what's truly important. You might put down this book and shed one of your weekly tasks: perhaps by hiring a cleaner for your home or someone to mow your lawn. Or you might decide to park a project that is giving you sleepless nights for little return. The best way to climb a mountain is to take small steps.

As you begin to make changes in your life and put your intentions and ideas into action, you will gradually remove the limitations that are holding you back – whether you have put those limitations on yourself or you've allowed others to impose them. You will realize that the one person in control of *your* life is *you*. It's up to you whether you want to keep all those plates spinning at the same time, or let one rest for a while, or even drop it altogether. If you want to find more time for your family, write a book or take the leap and start your own business: you *can* do it. Anything is possible when you stop trying to do everything at once.

When less is better

To simplify a little and focus on your priorities doesn't diminish your life; it makes it better. I used to think that 'mindfulness' was something people used as an excuse to be lazy until I realized that *appearing* productive – filling every moment of the day with tasks and activities – is not the same as *being* productive. 'Presenteeism' isn't the same as being present and fully focused.

When we embrace the 'less is more' attitude to life, work and everything in between, we appreciate all the good things we already have. We gather the courage to prune our lives of things and people that aren't so good for us in order that we can grow. When you begin truly to value your time, you have the space in which to identify exciting new opportunities, rather than being weighed down by all those commitments you've agreed to take on when your heart and your gut were crying out 'NO THANK YOU'. You become an expert in what you're really good at and passionate about, rather than a jack of all trades and master of none.

> *When you stop trying to do so much,*
> *you get so much more done.*

How to use this book

This is your book, so it's about you getting the best out of your life, not someone else's.

To make a successful change and begin to achieve more by doing less, you first need to take stock. You need to evaluate exactly what's currently missing or undervalued and what you want out of your life. And you need to recognize what is coming between you and the things that really matter; whether that's success, relationships, health or financial freedom.

All too often, it is fear that keeps us stuck in our patterns. If we're super busy then *of course* we must be doing OK: no one can point to us and say we're not working hard. Our culture has normalized being stressed, frazzled, running on empty.

THE 'LESS IS MORE' APPROACH TO LIFE

BEING FULLY PRESENT IN WHATEVER YOU'RE DOING,
AND WHOMEVER YOU'RE WITH

ABLE TO RECOGNIZE THE OPPORTUNITIES THAT REAP
THE BEST REWARDS

DOING THE RIGHT THING, AT THE RIGHT TIME

DOING WHAT YOU LOVE, AND LOVING WHAT YOU DO

TRUSTING IN YOURSELF AND YOUR INSTINCTS

TRUSTING IN OTHERS, BEING WILLING AND ABLE
TO ASK FOR HELP

ACHIEVING MORE OF WHAT MATTERS IN LESS TIME

KNOWING WHAT'S IMPORTANT AND WHEN TO LET GO

MAKING THE MOST OF YOUR TALENTS AND ABILITIES

ENJOYING EVERY STEP OF THE WAY

But deep down we sense there might be another, more enjoyable and more *productive* way. We know that if we had the courage of our convictions and followed our true passions then we would break out of the trap. The lesson here is always to be open to moments of transformation; it is often when life feels scary that the biggest breakthroughs will come.

Once you begin to understand that our biggest opportunities may lie within our fears, then you can start to look at fear differently, as something to be embraced and unravelled rather than hidden from or ignored.

The next step is to understand what is important to you and your happiness. This isn't always as easy as we might think, because most of us have been conditioned from an early age to 'know' what we should and shouldn't want. If you're a parent, you'll appreciate the almost instantaneous guilt you feel the moment you take a second to breathe, let alone take a whole day for yourself. This isn't about what your parents, partner, friends or children want for you or what they think you should want for yourself. This is about what *you* want and what you need to change or stop doing in order to get it. To be the best parent, partner or friend when the plane is going down you need to put your own oxygen mask on first.

Once you're clear on *what* you want, I'll show you how to **filter**, **prune**, **prioritize** and **focus**. These are some of the productivity tools that enable you to achieve much more in less time. You need to identify what really matters first to make the tools super effective.

It's a chain reaction – recognize where you are, see where you want to be and then work out the best and quickest route to get there. Who can you ask for help? What tasks can you outsource or delegate? What are the important deadlines you need to meet? What skills, knowledge or experience do you need to finish what you start? What can you stop doing? What can you say no to more often, so that you have more time to say yes to the things that matter?

The world is full of opportunities, but sometimes the best opportunity is to learn to filter out the most important, meaningful ones. That way, you can give them 100 per cent of your attention, nail them, and then be able to lead a fulfilled life, not just a productive one.

Do the right thing at the right time, rather than trying to do everything all of the time.

STUCK IN THE CYCLE OF BUSYNESS WHILE NOT DOING THE THINGS YOU REALLY WANT?

STOP. LOOK CLOSELY. SEE YOUR REASONS TO BE BUSY FOR WHAT THEY REALLY ARE – LESS FEAR, MORE HONESTY

FILTER
IDENTIFY WHAT AND WHO IS IMPORTANT

PRUNE
LET GO OF WHAT ISN'T IMPORTANT

PRIORITIZE
BRING WHAT MATTERS IN YOUR LIFE TO THE FRONT OF THE QUEUE

FOCUS
DO WHAT YOU LOVE AND DO IT REALLY WELL

PART ONE:
WHEN DID LIFE GET SO COMPLICATED?

‘ *Life is really simple, but we insist on making it complicated.* ’

Confucius

Is your life how you imagined it would be, or is the reality more complicated and stressful than you planned? Do you get to the end of the day and wonder what you managed to achieve in between all the emails and phone calls, the endless meetings, the to-do list that just seems never to get done?

You hardly get a moment to yourself, you're *so busy* pushing ahead, but you're still not able to break through and be the person you really want to be. You're not getting the chance – you're constantly doing 'stuff' yet often struggle to finish what you start: there are just too many things vying for your attention.

Perhaps you have a great job but spend three hours every day commuting to the office and back, so that by the evening your spare time is just recovery time.

Maybe you're juggling being a parent with running a business or holding down a job, feeling that every day you spread yourself a little bit thinner and just don't have enough energy or attention to go round.

Or you might have managed to cut your commute to zero by going freelance, but don't know how to value your time or which potential projects will give you the best return. Instead, you end up trying to pitch for everything.

You might love taking on new challenges, and have fresh and exciting ideas every day of the week, but you don't have time to see them through to fruition. Now you're struggling even to know which is the right opportunity to focus on.

Or you'd love the luxury of following what your heart tells you, but you're more concerned right now with paying the mortgage and keeping your job. The idea of doing less fills you with dread that everything will simply fall apart.

You might be trying to make your mark in your industry or company, being the 'go to' person your manager always relies on. How can you stand out from the crowd unless you are ever the willing volunteer?

It feels like there isn't any time left to think, to wander in the park or just sit by the water. To 'just sit' is a luxury you

28

can't afford, and even on the odd occasions when you do, a tumble of thoughts about all the things you haven't managed to do come crashing in and make true relaxation impossible.

We have so many opportunities today that sometimes, what started out as a sweet-shop of choices begins to turn into a workhouse of chores under the pressure to be everything to everyone, to be professionally successful and an amazing parent, to be the first into the office and the last to leave, to be in three places at once, and to be not just dependable but indispensable.

Busyness has become equated with productivity, but the opposite is true. Every time you are distracted from one task by something or someone else it takes on average eleven minutes to get your focus back. Conversely, if you try to concentrate on one piece of work for longer than ninety minutes without taking a break, you are actually likely to be unproductive – you could be recharging your energy with a wander outside. Saying yes to every request so that you become the 'go to' person isn't best for you or anyone else; instead, you end up spreading yourself too thin and taking on tasks that others could do better.

1. STUCK IN THE BUSY TRAP

❛ If I was always busy and I managed to avoid wiping out, sooner or later, everything would work out. ❜

Seth Godin

It's all too easy to get trapped in a cycle of anxiety (or boredom) and 'busyness'. We're not sure if it's even a good idea to try and step off the hamster wheel, let alone whether we might have enough courage or energy to do so. It's like a bad relationship – you know it's not right, but the alternative seems worse. That is fear – fear of the unknown. So we come up with lots of seemingly logical reasons why we have no option but to keep doing the things we wouldn't choose to in our 'ideal' life.

Reasons to be fearful – how many apply to you?

- ☐ I take on too much
- ☐ I find it hard to say no
- ☐ I can't decide what's the most important thing so I try to do everything
- ☐ I'm scared of the important things, they're more risky so I keep busy doing everything else
- ☐ I'm juggling family and work and spreading myself too thin
- ☐ My to-do list is never ending
- ☐ I don't want to miss out on anything
- ☐ You've got to be seen to be busy; I wouldn't want anyone to think I'm lazy

- ☐ I need to keep this job to pay the bills, so I'm first in and last out every day
- ☐ I'm not the boss, I don't get to choose how I spend my time
- ☐ I spend so long commuting that it leaves no time to enjoy myself
- ☐ Taking time for myself feels selfish
- ☐ I'm answering emails and calls all hours of the day and even on my holidays

And how's that working out for you?

- ☐ I feel anxious for much of the time
- ☐ I'm stressed out
- ☐ I'm filling my day with things that don't really interest or motivate me
- ☐ I don't do things to the best of my ability
- ☐ I'm not fulfilling my potential
- ☐ I've forgotten how to have fun
- ☐ I've forgotten how to relax, my mind is always on the go
- ☐ I feel stuck in a pattern I can't get out of
- ☐ I put things off; I'm always procrastinating even though I'm so busy
- ☐ I feel overwhelmed
- ☐ I don't give people or tasks my full attention
- ☐ I've lost sight of what really matters

31

Are you putting your own dreams to the back of the queue?

I love to write. It is a powerful outlet for creativity and ideas and provides a medium to connect with new people. It's one of my greatest joys. Yet if you looked back at my blog a couple of years ago it might have given the distinct impression that I was trying to avoid it.

That is one of the perils of modern-day life. How do we do everything when our to-do list seems never ending? How do we decipher the important from the urgent? How do we take care of our responsibilities while ensuring the things that make our heart sing aren't pushed to the back of the queue?

The back of the queue never seems to get to the front …

I'm not going to pretend it's simple or that I've got it all sussed. I haven't. But I've certainly woken up to the fact that if I don't do the things I love, everything else seems like a chore.

When I put the things and people I love to the back of the queue, the result is that I feel flat, drained and off my game. How does working like this benefit me? It doesn't. Nor does it benefit anyone else.

In order to operate at our peak, like athletes we need to feed and nurture our whole selves, not just the part that works and makes money. By doing so, we will solve challenges faster, get more creative, be more inspired and produce better results. We'll also be happier, healthier and more fun to be around. Win–win.

Now that I've created time and space for writing, my blog is far from the 'luxury' I might have mislabelled it a few years ago. It's my chance to connect with people and create new and fruitful partnerships. There is usually a very good reason we love the things we do. These are the things that lead to both success and happiness – if we just give them a chance.

Seeing the wood for the trees

When we are caught in the busy trap, it's incredibly hard to see a way out. We might dream of a life where it's possible to just quit our job or take a sabbatical, even leave on time once in a while to pick up our kids from school. But what if you're working all hours to pay for the mortgage, what else can you really do? Is it possible to make real life more ideal? At this point it's difficult to believe you could stop even for a moment to work out what you want, let alone make those things a priority.

The only way we can begin to see more clearly, and see another way, is to give ourselves space. It might only be five minutes before beginning our work day . . . and yes, every one of us can find five minutes if we want to.

Those minutes are yours, to look at your life and yourself,

33

to appreciate all the good things. Ask yourself a simple question: if there was one thing you could do today if you had no fear or distractions or excuses, what would it be?

STOP. The world won't end. Often your 'busyness' just creates more confusion. You need clarity, and to get that you have to stop and take yourself out of your usual routine, even for just a day.

FOCUS on getting just ONE area of your life where you feel out of control back in control. Instead of spreading your efforts thinly, concentrate on just one thing. One thing will lead to another.

ASK for help. Just remember, it's always easier to find solutions for other people and to offer help to them. So in turn let someone else help you.

These are the three simple things I want you to take from this book and keep for whenever you need them, for whenever life is getting in the way of the things and the people that matter.

Retreat and reflect

On the battlefield, the best strategist will know when it is better to retreat and regroup rather than continually to push forward with no plan or purpose. As you read this book, give yourself just a few minutes in the day to pause and reflect on the ideas, what they mean to you and your life, and what you're going to do to make the change. Recharge your batteries and be ready to choose your moments rather than constantly trying to push yourself.

The guilt of responsibility

When you've got a mortgage to pay, family to support and co-workers who need your time, it feels a bit selfish to be focused on *your* life and what you need. This is a common problem for the many of us who suffer from the guilt of responsibility, but survival for your whole family requires you to take care of yourself first.

Think of your best moments, whether at home with your family or with your colleagues at work; think of the times you've really laughed or been united. Did you feel burdened then? And then think of the times you've done something particularly well, or been most successful. Were you doing

35

something you enjoy, that you are great at *and* have a passion for?

When you let the guilt of responsibility become too great, it weighs you down and slows you up so that you feel like you have even less time. Conversely, when we focus on the things that we are passionate about, the things that play to our strengths, shine a light on our talents and bring us joy, we get into a state of flow and become more productive than ever. In this state, we have the time to take proper care of not only ourselves but also those around us.

Sometimes we use our 'responsibilities' as the excuse for sticking with things as they are, when the reality is that it's our fear of failure that holds us back from taking a chance. If we keep busy every day then we can't blame ourselves for not pursuing our own dreams or ideas; there's just no time. This is when fear becomes like a comfort blanket and it's not easy to give it up.

The stress epidemic

A study published in the International Journal of Productivity and Performance Management *found that 40 per cent of work-related illness in the UK is caused by stress.*

Stress can be a contributing factor in:

heart disease	*anxiety*	*headaches*
weight gain	*premature ageing*	*insomnia*
depression	*IBS*	*suicide*

We've been conditioned to believe that a degree of stress is a good thing, it's a badge of honour that proves we must be working really hard, pushing to get the most out of life. Don't buy it. It's a myth. Studies show that stress lowers our productivity and it's the people who are happy in their work who get the most done and are more successful in the long run. Build a career that plays to your strengths and passions, focus on getting the results that really matter, find your flow and watch how much happier and more productive you become.

The disease to please

If you gain your sense of self worth from external validation (the need to be liked, respected, thanked or praised), then you may suffer from the disease to please, or in other words you just can't seem to say no. For some of the time, this seems to work out OK, you feel like the person everyone can rely on to get the job done; you'll be the shoulder to cry on, the family taxi service, cook, cleaner, baker and candlestick maker . . .

Many of us struggle with the concept that saying no can be a positive thing. What if we upset someone? What if they think we're not good enough? What if it's selfish or means we might miss an opportunity? Instead of learning to filter, we try to do everything and hope we'll be lucky enough to come across the good stuff along the way. But the reality is that we get so caught up with everybody else's business that our own dreams get pushed further and further into the background. We're not sure where to find them any more.

Once you see your 'busy' habits for what they are, which is usually a cover-up for underlying fear, patterns and conditioning, you can begin to shift your perspective. Give yourself the space to explore and understand what it is in your life that truly counts and what you need to do to fast track yourself to the front of the queue. Armed with understanding and desire, you can then develop your powers of filtering, including when to say no and when to say yes. You focus on the one thing that will make the biggest impact TODAY, that one phone call, that crafted pitch that could set up the rest of your year. Less trying to please everyone, more pleasing the people that count. Less trying to do everything, more doing what matters.

Keep it simple

Simplicity is the ultimate sophistication.

Leonardo da Vinci

Do you find that you sometimes seem to be struggling almost for the sake of struggling? You can't even think why any more but it feels impossible to do anything about it, especially when you are exhausted and depleted by the struggle itself.

It's time to get back to simply connecting with what motivates you. Simplicity is to be present in your life, in the here and now. Simplicity is being with people who inspire you and bring out the best in you; it's focusing on what you are doing right now, in the moment. It often feels like we don't have the luxury of choosing a simpler life, but there are always things in life and in our heads that we could choose to let go of in order to prioritize what's truly important.

'Busyness' is an addictive distraction. If you think you're too busy even to consider finding out what it is that you really want, let alone taking the steps to get there, you're wrong. Just stop watching TV for a week. Wake up an hour earlier. Start changing your priorities now and you will find the time.

The best thing about simplicity is how it has a way of giving us so much in the smallest of things. Simple pleasures bring the detail of life back into focus, rather than our constantly being on the search for more this, that or the other. Simplicity gives us room to think and breathe and refresh ourselves so that we have the time and energy to follow our goals and dreams – and just be. Slowing down can be the hardest thing of all, and yet it's essential nourishment for our soul, our creativity and our appreciation of life.

I'm not suggesting we sit around doing nothing all day. Personally, I couldn't think of anything worse; I find it hard enough to stay in bed beyond 6 a.m. even at the weekends. Instead, I like to think of it as an active slowdown.

There is a wonderful book called *Simplicity Parenting* by Kim John Payne. Not only is it an inspiration to all parents, but I think any adult can learn a thing or two from it about flourishing through simplicity in these increasingly busy times.

The book encourages you to streamline your home environment. Reduce the amount of toys, books and clutter it contains – as well as any bright lights, loud noise or other sensory overload. (This definitely applies to non-parents too.) Then it recommends that you establish rhythms and rituals. Schedule a break in the schedule. Our kids' lives are becoming a mini version of our own, filled with one appointment after the other, with no time to just be. Soccer clubs, tennis lessons, guitar, Mandarin, homework club, maths tuition, judo lessons . . . there are children who take as much as twelve hours of extra-curricular classes a week.

What happened to being a kid? Sure, some of those out-of-school activities are great fun, and adding a couple of lessons or sports to a child's week can be a good thing, but not if their time becomes so managed as to leave none for messing about and, well, playing. We could all benefit from less micro managing and more play.

< EXERCISE >

HOW ARE YOU SPENDING YOUR TIME?

➡ Look back, with the help of your diary, at what you did last week (if you were on holiday it doesn't count). Map everything: your work, evenings, early mornings, the people you saw, the tasks you tackled.

➡ Of all the things you did in the week, what gave you the highest return, both professionally and personally?

➡ When were you in flow and what were you doing?

➡ What was missing that you wish you'd done?

➡ What were the things you did that you really wished you had said no to?

➡ What were the things somebody else could have done, that you knew were too much to take on, which you resented or which turned out to be a waste of time?

2. HOW FEAR KEEPS US HOSTAGE

❛ We can easily forgive a child who is afraid of the dark; the real tragedy of life is when men are afraid of the light. ❜

Plato

Fear. It holds you back. It ties you down. It keeps us so busy that we never have a chance to step out of our comfort zone and see how life could really be. Fear eats away at our courage so that we spend all our time doing stuff we don't even really want to do: it is nearly always at the heart of our reasons, or rather our excuses, about why we're putting off our dreams. What if it all goes wrong? What if we're not good enough? What if I don't make enough money? What if I can never get another job? Fear doesn't just eat up the hours in the day; it fills our minds with so many thoughts that we no longer have the mental space or belief we need to turn our dreams into reality.

Is fear putting what's important to the back of the queue?

It's one of life's cruel ironies, but the things we want the most have more risks associated with them, because we care more about the outcome – and so even thinking about them makes us feel vulnerable. As a result, our minds will come up with every excuse or condition under the sun that means we can't focus on those things *right now*. It will be different when we have a chance to get our heads above water, when the children are grown up, when we win the lottery . . .

43

The 'when...then' trap

How many times have you heard people (maybe even yourself) say: 'I really want to X but I can't until I've done Y'? Do you recognize any of the following?

▶ 'I want to set up my own business, but I can't until my son goes to college.'
▶ 'I want to start applying for a promotion, but I can't until I've completed my master's.'
▶ 'I want to spend more time with my children/partner/ friends, but I can't until I've finished this project.'
▶ 'I want to launch my new product, but I can't until it's perfect.'
▶ 'I need to break up with my boyfriend, but I can't until we've sold our flat.'
▶ 'I want to give up smoking, but I'm too stressed.'
▶ 'I want to go running, but I can't until we move because my commute takes too long.'

This is how many of us justify not doing the things that we really want to do. Sure, they all *seem* like fair reasons for procrastinating – we're quite good at making things sound logical – but they are all based in fear. At the end of the day, the justifications we make are just our fears dressed up in better clothes. If we try for something that we truly care about and then fail to make it happen, won't we feel more hurt or a bigger failure? That's what many of us are programmed to believe, but it's another myth. I've never once regretted trying my best, even if things didn't turn out the way I had planned.

When we open up to life and its opportunities, we make deeper connections with ourselves and others, we learn vital lessons and have rich experiences.

Do you feel like there's something you want to do, or someone you want to be, but you're just not quite ready? Why are you putting it off? You know deep down what you want to go for, but there's that nagging little voice that says, 'Nearly . . . but not yet.' The truth is that we can't ever be 100 per cent ready. The perfect conditions don't exist and we can't control the outcome: we can only control our intentions and our efforts. We can't predict the future – and however prepared we think we might be there are always unexpected twists and turns just around the corner.

Have you ever considered how fearful over-thinking holds you back? Let's say there is a promotion you want to go for, but it's a couple of levels above your current position. It's a stretch, but you know you can do it. Then fear starts putting up obstacles in your mind. You start thinking about all the other candidates and how much more relevant experience they will have, how they will probably have better qualifications and a CV that puts yours in the shade. So you listen to motivational talks and read a few books to help change your way of thinking, but for a reason you can't put your finger on, you're still scared. It doesn't seem to be working. You don't want to embarrass yourself in front of your boss by applying for a position you're not going to get, so you sit staring at your computer screen and convince yourself: *I don't think I'm ready yet. I need another year or two's experience, then I'll be in a better position to apply.*

So you don't get the promotion. Not because you didn't

want it, and not because you weren't the best person for the job, but because you allowed fear to control your decision. You didn't want to step out of your comfort zone, and you couldn't muster up the self-belief to push yourself out of it.

If, instead, you had focused on the key things that would make you the perfect candidate for this promotion and chosen the one or two areas where you knew you excelled and could add real value to the company, you wouldn't have been distracted by the fearful talk in your head. You wouldn't have worried yourself out of trying because you would have been focused on the key things that made you right for the job.

The same thinking applies to any aspect of life, not just work. Imagine you're ten pounds overweight and know that you need to be doing something about it. You sit there after eating, pulling at your trousers to see if they've got any tighter. You think to yourself, *I really need to get fit. I want to start running.* Then, fear jumps back in and you start to create obstacles for yourself. *But it's winter and it's cold outside. I'll start tomorrow, but I've got that big project that needs to be done by Monday . . .* A series of overlapping conversations start running through your head: *Maybe it would be easier if I just did the no carb diet.* Or *I'll do a juice fast for a week, yeah, that's what I'll do, I'll juice for a week and then start exercising. Oh, but I've got a ton of client lunch meetings next week, I can't juice then. I'll start the week after. I'll just have smaller portions and cut out the sweet stuff.* Then you start feeling tired and think: *I really need another coffee, and something sweet to give me energy.* Now, you're lost. Fear has won.

Sound familiar? You don't lose any weight because you're

putting your own barriers in the way, waiting for the elusive 'perfect moment' to arrive. Instead of focusing on the one or two areas you could change immediately that would help you lose weight, you start thinking of all the reasons you can't. You convince yourself that until you're less busy, there's no point even attempting small changes. So, you stay stuck.

It's time to get unstuck

The voice that tells you you're not ready is the voice of fear in another guise. The voice you need to listen to is the instinctive one that says, **this is the right thing to do**. Changing a habit or a whole way of life is never going to be easy, so you might never feel completely and utterly ready. Go ahead and take a small step anyway. You don't have to make an almighty leap from where you are today to the fulfilment of all your dreams. You don't have to be perfect, you don't have to turn your back on all the good stuff you already have in your life. It's a step: try something, do one thing.

If a lack of practical skills stands between where you are now and where you want to be, there's nothing to stop you acquiring those skills other than a fear of the unknown, or that you might make the wrong choice. What if I study to gain those extra skills then change my mind? I will have wasted all that time and money. Wrong. Learning new skills is never a waste of time or money, even if you don't put them to good use straight away.

If you're waiting for all the planets to align and for the conditions to be perfect before you go ahead and do

47

something you've been dreaming about all your life, you're letting the gremlins of resistance that live in your head win the day. It's time to turn the tables.

> ❛ *The opposite of fear is love – love of the challenge, love of the work, the pure joyous passion to take a shot at our dream and see if we can pull it off.* ❜
>
> Steven Pressfield, *Do the Work*

What are you afraid of?

These are a selection of answers to a question I posted on Facebook (so yes, Facebook does have its uses). I asked: 'What are the fears that have held you back that you wish you could have conquered sooner? There is no such thing as a stupid fear (for the record I'm petrified of sharks and it's stopped me diving).'

- ► 'Upsetting the happy apple cart – the status quo that everyone's used to.'
- ► 'Being laughed at, that people won't like me, you know, the story about ourselves we buy into.'
- ► 'Any kind of experience where I have to fully let go and TRUST.'
- ► 'Of honesty, of upsetting others.'
- ► 'Regret.'
- ► 'Of failure, which stops me from even starting something new.'
- ► 'Of taking risks and making the wrong choice.'

- ► 'Life stopping short.'
- ► 'Running out of time.'
- ► 'Not making my mark.'
- ► 'Losing my house.'
- ► 'Not being a good mum.'
- ► 'Criticism.'
- ► 'Being loved.'
- ► 'Being alone.'
- ► 'Not being accepted.'
- ► 'Not being seen, not being heard.'
- ► 'Not being good enough.'
- ► 'Messing up the good things in my life.'
- ► 'Being found out to be a fraud.'
- ► 'I'm a control freak, if I can't guarantee the outcome, I'm scared what might happen.'

All of these fears sow seeds of doubt or just distract us from getting on with what we want to do. They fill our minds with so much anxiety that we feel paralysed. Even a fear as seemingly solid as that of losing our house or job is partly a trap of our own making. Staying in a job to pay the bills is never the only choice. We can take steps in the evenings or on the weekends towards creating a bridge to a new career or starting up a business of our own, without taking on financial risk. You can start making and implementing a simple plan today that doesn't jeopardize what is already good in your life: it will just give you the focus you need to make it even better.

Lots of our fears are based in comparison or perceptions. How we look to others, whether we'll be good enough, whether we'll be accepted and liked. We forget that when we are true to ourselves we are naturally all of those things, because we're being the person we were meant to be. When we embrace the 'Less is More' attitude to life, we realize that the only things that matter are the things that matter.

The trouble is that fear eats away at our confidence. We're not sure we can trust our own choices or decisions; what if we follow our dreams and they fall apart, won't that feel so much worse than making do and making busy? Hell no.

Fear and self-sabotage

Sometimes the fear of changing your life for the better is so strong that you will actively beat a path to failure instead. I know it sounds crazy, but really smart people do this. That way you can't be in trouble – you convince yourself that you'd end up failing anyway, so why put yourself through the heartache of daring to believe you might make something amazing happen, only to be proved right? It's like a self-destruct button.

This often happens when we want to make lifestyle changes, such as stopping smoking or getting fit. It's akin to going to a spa or gym with a suitcase full of secret chocolates; it makes no sense but it's an easy trap to fall into. It can be the same in any area of life, from thinking perhaps we're just not meant to be in a great, loving relationship to worrying every day at work that however much experience and knowledge we have in our field, at any moment we will be 'found out' as not coming up to scratch.

When we sabotage our own efforts, it is often because

we don't quite believe in our hearts that we are up for the challenge ahead. We are afraid, deep down, that we aren't good enough. Our minds react to this fear by coming up with all manner of negative, self-sabotaging reasons not to bother being brave or making a change; we'll be safer just staying right where we are.

You can't turn off such negative thoughts with the flick of a switch. If only it were that easy. But you can begin to notice them and choose how to respond and react. As you identify what brings you your greatest joy and fulfilment in Part Two, you will naturally start to focus on the more positive things in your life and have greater confidence to use your fears as signals for growth, rather than challenges to avoid.

< EXERCISE >
ESCAPE THE 'WHEN . . . THEN' TRAP

➡ Think of something you have been putting off because of a condition (excuse) you believe makes it impossible to start.

➡ Now, instead of jumping straight to the end goal, think of one practical step you can take towards it. Stop waiting to be 'ready', just start.

➡ Before you turn the page, what can you do right now to start? Do it.

Peeling back the layers

Most people will have a number of roles they play in life. It might be the 'always happy person who gets on with everyone', or the 'confident business person'. These roles are certainly a part of you, but there might be other aspects that are currently hidden and you'd like to bring out. However, you worry that if you let down your guard you'll feel too exposed.

One of the most viewed TED Talks, by Brené Brown, is titled 'The Power of Vulnerability'. As a researcher, Brown wanted to find out what truly 'connected' people had in common, and she discovered they had a shared willingness to be open to vulnerability. This openness allowed them to make deep personal connections, because the places where we experience feelings of fear and vulnerability are the same places where we will find our dreams, along with incredible experiences of love and joy.

When we are truly honest with ourselves and with others we are vulnerable; when you open yourself up to the possibilities of life you open yourself up to being hurt, but you also get to experience times of growth. Rather than use fear to fuel your excuses for being busy, allow it to give you insight into what's really important to you. Then you can prune away the things that are weighing you down or getting between you and the heart of life.

Each of us has labels with which we describe ourselves or have been described by others. Some are useful while others hold us back and stop us from reaching out for opportunities that we know in our hearts we desire. Do you recognize any of these labels, and if you do, put them to the 'useful' test. If any of your self-beliefs are preventing you from growing or doing what you love, now is the time to begin to let them go.

► 'I've always been the boring one.'
► 'I'm shy.'
► 'I can't stand being wrong.'
► 'I'm never wrong.'
► 'I'm not a "group" person.'
► 'I'm not good on my own.'

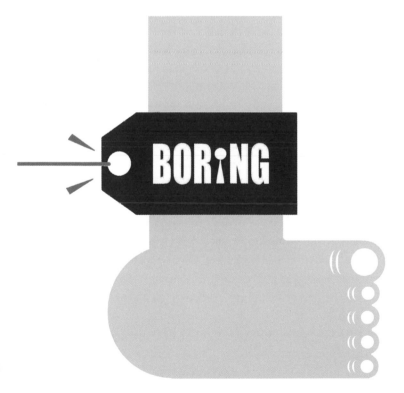

Do the beliefs you have about yourself, or how you think other people see you, hold you back? Maybe you're like me and think that you don't have any limiting beliefs. All I'd ask you to do is to take a hard look at why there are things that you want to do, but you're not doing them. I bet, no matter how crazy it might seem, there is a belief behind it.

Sometimes we get stuck with beliefs that aren't even true any longer. For example many children labelled 'shy' believe as adults that they are unable to talk confidently to new people or make a presentation; in fact there have probably been many occasions on which they have done all those things without realizing it. It's just that nobody ever told them that introverts can be confident, too.

For years I assumed that I wasn't held back by any limiting beliefs – whether my own or others'. I was adamant that those were not my issues. I'd fought hard to succeed against all odds, it was my mindset that got me through, so there was no way I had limiting beliefs.

Then, while taking a short break with a friend, talking about the future in a way you really only do on holiday, I shared how much I love to write. I talked about how my career had started as a result of writing for *Cosmopolitan* and how I had wanted to write a book ever since I'd travelled across Mexico at eighteen. My friend asked why I hadn't pursued writing as a career. My unthinking reply? 'You can't make real money by being creative, or at least not creating content.'

WHOA! Really? I didn't see that one coming. I wonder

what my belief system would have been if Steven Spielberg had been my dad? All I've ever wanted to do is to create content that inspires, engages and empowers people to be their true selves. I've waited this long to do it because of a long-held and grossly incorrect belief that it wasn't possible to do this and make money – despite the fact that within seconds of my reply to my friend I could think of at least thirty people who had created a life of financial freedom by doing exactly that.

When I finally gave myself permission to be honest, I realized that I had always looked to people who ran 'real' businesses as being successful. Anyone who did anything else was either a 'corporate' or 'lacked ambition'. What an insane notion, yet I'd lived with it for years and let it affect virtually every major decision in my life. I had spent years climbing the ladder of success, but it was leaning up the wrong wall. Doh! I've got some catching up to do.

Take this opportunity for your own reality check. Everyone has a belief that is holding them back, but you might not always recognize it. Be willing and prepared to *dig deeper* beyond the surface to get to who you really want to be.

Your self-beliefs are so powerful. You can use all the experiences in your life to shake you up in a positive way, or you can store them up as negative excuses for not taking chances. It's up to you whether to dwell on the negatives or focus on the positives, on the opportunities you have right now or that you can create with the skills you have at your fingertips and the passion in your heart.

< EXERCISE >

LESS FIXED, MORE FLEXIBLE

Dr Ilona Boniwell, one of the world leaders in the field of positive psychology, described how people tend to have either a 'fixed mindset' or a 'growth mindset'. Her research discovered this often has to do with how we were taught at school or parented.

If, as a child, you were praised more often for getting things right, then you might have developed a more fixed mindset. When things are going well, then all is good in your world; the trouble starts when you hit a setback. You might find you have a tendency towards an all-or-nothing mentality in this situation – success or failure. This is because you believe your abilities and talents are fixed, so if you fail first time round you will often want to give up immediately and do something else.

If, however, you were praised for your efforts as a child, you will tend to have a growth mindset. Failure isn't an immediate trigger to abandon ship, it's just an indication that you need to learn from the situation or try a new approach. Flexibility is inbuilt as you enjoy the process of finding out how to make something work as much as the end result.

With a fixed mindset, over time we can start to back out on ourselves even as we approach a challenge; the voice of fear inside starts questioning, 'Are you sure you can do it? What if you fail, how will you feel then? What will everyone else think of you?' As soon as things get tough a person with a fixed mindset will often think to themselves, 'What's the point? I knew it. Now I just feel stupid so I'll get out while I can.' It's very difficult to take criticism when your mind is in fixed mode. Constructive feedback sounds like, 'I'm really disappointed in you. You're clearly not capable.' Either that or you reject any criticism: 'It's not my fault, who do they think they are?'

You can actually train your brain to be less fixed and develop a growth mindset instead.

➡ Know that you can't get everything right, but every day is an opportunity to learn something new and get better at something that matters to you.

➡ Practise using growth mindset language:

- 'I'm not sure how to do this right now, but I'm willing to learn or ask for help.'
- 'If I don't get it right, I'm not a failure. Look at all the successful people who have overcome setbacks. Failure is a chance for growth.'
- 'If I don't try, I'll never learn anything.'

➡ Listen fully to constructive feedback or criticism and use it as it is meant, to help you grow.

3. CHANGING THE HABITS OF A LIFETIME

❝ To dare is to lose one's footing momentarily.
Not to dare is to lose oneself. ❞

Søren Kierkegaard

Like a new pair of shoes, change is good for you, even if it isn't immediately comfortable. You might think that if you stay where you are, then at least you won't run the risk of setting yourself up to fail or be judged by others. You know that things could be better, but what if you rock the boat and make everything worse? You know you're struggling to manage everything right now, but you haven't got the luxury to take a step back and figure it out.

The truth is that just beyond your comfort zone is the place where you grow as a person. Where you are truly honest about what's important to you, where you stretch yourself and you give things a go for the first time. Yes, it can be a scary place, but excitingly scary too. It's where you are creative, daring and free.

To stay in your comfort zone is like putting on a straitjacket. You can't move. And the thing is, however much you might think that staying in familiar surroundings will ensure security, the reality is the opposite. You end up feeling like you're always running, but never getting anywhere.

Who knows where life will take you if you just lose the straitjacket? That's the fun part.

IF IT AIN'T BROKE, DON'T FIX IT...
BUT WHAT IF THERE'S A *BETTER* WAY
OF DOING IT?

DON'T UPSET THE APPLE CART...
BUT WHAT IF THEY'RE ROTTEN?

KEEP YOUR HEAD DOWN...
BUT THEN YOU CAN'T SEE THE LIGHT.

Less fear, more freedom

risk: a situation involving exposure to danger, the possibility that something unpleasant or unwelcome will happen

chance: an opportunity to do or achieve something, the probability of something pleasant happening

If you see everything new and unknown as a risk, you won't be very likely to take a chance or grab that opportunity right in front of you.

My son is a year younger than the daughter of one of my best friends. We had a laugh when my friend's daughter was about to learn to ride a bike but felt scared because she didn't have any stabilizers. 'Don't worry,' my son assured her, 'I'll show you how to do it.' Thing is, he'd never ridden a bike before in his life but he saw a chance to do something new and exciting.

Most of us will remember learning to ride a bike with one of our parents holding on to the back of it and then, at some point, they let go. Yes, we probably fell over a few times, we might even have got a few cuts and grazes, but what a feeling it was to go sailing off through the park or along the driveway even for a few moments.

❛ *Three times as many children are taken to hospital each year after falling out of bed as [after] falling out of trees.* ❜

Stephen Moss, 'Natural Childhood'

Child psychologists are discovering that because parents are becoming so overly protective of children that the children are ending up hurting themselves more often, and the radius of 'their world' is getting smaller and smaller – for many it hardly goes beyond the front door. When children are allowed to climb trees at a young age they learn how to fall; they become more resilient. In our valiant attempts to 'protect' our children we have labelled any risk as potentially harmful; that has thwarted opportunities for them to learn and grow into their own independent selves.

This over-protective streak is affecting our adult experiences too. I recently drove to my local recycling centre, parked and was promptly told I must turn my car to face the other way because people 'weren't allowed to walk behind their cars'.

This has spilled over into denting our confidence when it comes to trying new experiences or new ways of doing things. But how many of your best moments in life came from being too careful? And what about the times when you took a deep breath and you took a chance, on love, on a new job, on starting a business, moving to a new house or even country? What about the feeling when you tried something you never thought you'd have the guts to do?

I had always been afraid of diving; of not knowing what is out there in the sea beyond my field of vision. My imagination would run away with itself – I couldn't cope with the thought of there being a shark swimming behind me. When I finally decided to *just let go* and took the plunge, I discovered a world I could never have imagined. It was so beautiful and peaceful. Taking what felt to me like a risk made it all the more magical.

You may be laughing at the absurdity of this, but remember fear is relative – it's all in the eyes of the beholder. The more you think about your fears, the bigger they become, so that you will soon have all of the worst case scenarios covered (I was going to be eaten alive by Jaws) and you will have succeeded in stopping yourself before you have even started.

It's the same in our careers and businesses; we can keep our heads down, keep busy and hope that nobody notices us because that way no one will ask any awkward questions – or we can take a chance and decide to shine, to do what makes our hearts sing. It's normal not to want to 'put yourself out there', where you might get judged, criticized, make a fool of yourself, be rejected. This is why it's a great idea to practise letting go of your own judgements and criticism towards both yourself and others. Does it really matter what people think of you, or does it really matter what you do? And if you do what you do authentically, then you will automatically navigate your way towards those in your natural tribe, as in the people who 'get you'.

Worry less, and be more.

❝ *We must be willing to fail and to appreciate
the truth that often life is not a problem to be solved,
but a mystery to be lived.* ❞

M. Scott Peck

Small acts of bravery

The good news is that the moment you take even the smallest step towards something that you would like to have in your life, this is the moment you begin to embrace your fear and discover your inner courage. The original meaning of the word *courage* was 'to act from the heart'. To live a courageous life doesn't mean that you never have any fear, but you are strong enough in your heart to face your fears rather than hide away from them.

The most important thing, wherever you are on the fear scale, is to do something different with your day and take a step towards where you want to be. People think that we only conquer fear in leaps and bounds, but it is the smaller steps that create a courageous way of life.

Sometimes, life will throw you a huge challenge that will force the courageous person in you to appear, but you can also practise small acts of bravery in your everyday life. Making a phone call that you've been putting off for weeks, that's an act of bravery. Asking for help with something you're not sure how to get done, that's definitely an act of bravery. Saying hello to that person who caught your eye across the room. That might seem trivial, but for many people those acts can be quite daunting.

It takes practice, but if you are willing to change your perspective, your fears will become a source of inspiration and adventure rather than a scary, no-go area. I know people who were too shy to even talk to someone they didn't know, yet now they speak to crowds with charisma. I know people who were scared to give up their jobs, and now run fantastically successful businesses.

When you feel fear, you are on the threshold of something great. When you step through fear, there is always love on the other side.

PART TWO:
WHAT REALLY MATTERS

❝ *Ester asked why people are sad.*

"That's simple," says the old man. "They are the prisoners of their personal history. Everyone believes that the main aim in life is to follow a plan. They never ask if that plan is theirs or if it was created by another person. They accumulate experiences, memories, things, other people's ideas, and it is more than they can possibly cope with. And that is why they forget their dreams." ❞

Paulo Coelho, *The Zahir*

If we're going to achieve more by doing less, then we have to understand what really matters to us. We need to know what is holding us back or keeping us so busy we have no time left for what's important.

Now is the time to get personal and decide what really makes you happy. It doesn't have to be complicated. It might be staring you right in the face. One thing I can guarantee, it will require you doing less of the stuff that doesn't matter, so you have the time to focus on what does.

As the old man in *The Zahir* says, we often end up following someone else's plan in life and not our own. We spend so much of life doing what we think we should do and what other people think we should do, rather than what we really want.

When we were kids our dreams were filled with infinite possibilities. We wanted to be firefighters, astronauts or singers. We wanted to explore jungles, climb mountains and sail the seven seas. Then as we got a bit older we started to take on the expectations of others around us: our parents, our teachers, friends and family. You're good at maths, so you're encouraged to be an accountant; the fact that writing is what really makes you happy is cast aside. Most people mean well. They want the 'best' for you; but what they believe is best is based on their own set of beliefs and the ones they inherited from *their* parents, teachers, partners and society. It all seems so logical . . . to them.

We are surrounded by expectations. We have an idea of 'success' that has little to do with our heart and everything to do with our status. You might be so determined to live up to or exceed your parents' or your own expectations that you drive yourself day and night to get there, only to miss everything you're passing by along the way.

When you begin to follow your own dreams, your need for approval diminishes; you spend far less time worrying about what others might think of you and more time getting on with doing what you love, with the people you love.

How often do you feel you've spent the whole day 'maxed out', yet at the end of it you have achieved very little? If we're really going to start living, we have to take stock and understand exactly what we want so we can make our own plan to go out and get it. This isn't about trying to obtain the things we think we should want; this is about our real, heartfelt desires. At a time when we are bombarded with demands, it is even more important to filter and focus. It's time to prune what's holding you back, then prioritize the things that will create the life you dream of.

Put aside any existing expectations and ask yourself afresh, 'What do I want to do with my life?' When what you do matches up with what you really want, you become the type of person who is happy, successful and can make a difference to the world around you. When you are aligned with your purpose, you no longer drag your heels on the way to work, you get masses done and you're a really nice person to be around.

*It might be self-serving to do what you enjoy,
but it isn't selfish.*

At first, you might feel vulnerable – it's one thing to worry about not living up to other people's expectations, but the thought of failing to realize your own dreams can be so great it stops you from taking the chance. Better to know your limits and not get too big for your boots or you might just be setting yourself up for a major fall. But when you live life on your own terms and you make a mistake, you realize there is no point in worrying about being blamed or criticized – you just focus on what you need to do next. That's truly liberating.

*To remember who you are, forget who
everybody said you were.*

Stop making do with making busy

❮ *What is the pot of gold that justifies spending the best years of your life hoping for happiness in the last?* ❯
Tim Ferriss

Remember that happiness statistic? The majority of people are happiest before the age of twenty-five and after sixty-five, so for the forty years in between we're stuck in a state of 'making do' in the hope that happiness will reappear when we retire (which is also getting later and later). In 2008, *USA Today* published a survey on how people's perception of time and their use of it had changed over a decade. Every year from

69

1987 to 2008, respondents reported being 'busier'. Asked what they were sacrificing for their busyness, 30 per cent said family, 44 per cent friends, 52 per cent recreation and 56 per cent sleep.

How and when did being busy take precedence over friends and family? What is the real value of being so busy we can't even take holidays? There are no rules that tell us we have to live according to the statistics, we can all be outliers if we want to be, we just have to start making deliberate choices concerning our lives and our priorities. The more we can identify our own sources of happiness, joy and meaning, the more we align what we do with what we love.

The most successful people do exactly that; they don't put off happiness or wait for it to come to them. They actively seek what makes them tick. They prune and filter and stop worrying so much about all the things they *should* do, which gives them the time and energy they need to do what they *want* to do.

Don't settle for discomfort

Watch a child at play and you'll never cease to be amazed by the capacity of their imaginations and their creativity. They know exactly what it is to dream big and be constantly in wonder of both the world and their own place in it. As we get older we realize there are healthy limits to behaviour; the trouble is that we place the same limitations on our imaginations and our dreams (we should know our own limitations and work within them; if the dreams don't happen we will end up a failure, etc.). But without big dreams, we have nothing to strive for. We stay right where we are, stuck for ever wondering 'what if . . . ?'

It's easy to get used to the environment we're in, whatever that has become and even if it isn't healthy for us. A frog placed into boiling water will jump straight out, but if it's in cold water and the heat is very gradually increased, the frog will stay there and eventually die. In small ways, we allow something similar to happen in our own lives all the time. The job that no longer has any joy in it for us but pays the bills, the relationship that has gone sour but that we somehow can't seem to extricate ourselves from, eating the wrong foods when we know in our hearts we want to be healthy and full of energy – taking action, even letting hurtful things go, seems to be more painful than 'making do'.

If you are ever stuck in this type of situation or pattern of thinking, then look at the labels you use to describe yourself. Why are you accepting these limitations? Why are you holding on to your baggage?

Stop labelling yourself as one thing or the other and open yourself to all the possibilities that are already within you and still to come. What can you do differently?

❧ *If you haven't found it yet, keep looking. Don't settle. As with all matters of the heart, you'll know when you find it.* ❧

Steve Jobs

♥

MEDIOCRE BECOMES EXCEPTIONAL
WHEN YOU:

ASK YOURSELF WHAT YOU REALLY
WANT AND WHAT'S IMPORTANT
IDENTIFY YOUR STRENGTHS
AND PASSIONS
INCREASINGLY BRING THESE
INTO WHAT YOU DO
IDENTIFY WHAT'S HOLDING
YOU BACK
INCREASINGLY LET THESE GO

♥

4. THE MORE MYTH

❛ The secret of happiness, you see, is not found in seeking more, but in developing the capacity to enjoy less. ❜

Socrates

Are you really happy? What does that even mean? Society conditions us to believe that if we accumulate the trappings – a good job, nice home, partner, family – we will feel fulfilled. If that's the case, why are so many of us asking, 'Is this it?' If you are asking the question, then the answer is 'no'.

Most of us have been conditioned in the culture of 'more, more, more' when it comes to success and happiness. More money, more clothes, more food, more gadgets. The problem is that now we're feeling overloaded and overwhelmed. We eat too much, drink too much, work too much and spend too much. As people in the wealthiest countries have become richer, their health has deteriorated inversely: heart disease, diabetes and depression – the diseases of the 'more' culture – have become epidemic. It's time to think about replacing more with less, but better.

The Mexican fisherman and the banker

An investment banker was on holiday in Mexico and visiting a tiny fishing village on the coast when he spotted a small boat mooring in the harbour. On board were one fisherman and his catch of a few large, gleaming fish. They got chatting and the banker said he was very impressed by the quality of the fish; he asked how long it took to catch them.

'Just a little while,' said the fisherman.

The banker asked why he didn't stay out longer to catch more fish, and the fisherman said that he didn't need to. He'd caught enough to support his family, and would spend the rest of the day with his wife and children, enjoy a siesta, walk to the village cantina and play music with his friends in the evening over a few drinks.

The banker wasn't impressed, saying the fisherman was wasting a great opportunity to make money. He could go out for longer, catch more fish, then use the proceeds to buy a bigger boat, in time even building up to a fleet. Once the business was big enough he would be able to move to the city, deal direct with the processors rather than through middle men, and run the business from an office instead of having to go out on the water every day.

The fisherman asked, 'How long will all this take, señor?' and the banker estimated it would take maybe twenty years, but by that time he would have such a successful business he'd be able to sell it and become very rich.

'And what would I do then?'

'Well, you'd retire. You could move to a small fishing village by the sea where you can sleep in, play with your grandkids, fish a little, spend time with your wife, and in the evenings walk to the village cantina and play music with your friends over a few drinks.'

What is *your* secret to happiness?

Study after study tries to determine what makes people happy. But however much scientists, philosophers or gurus try to pin happiness down, the truth is we are all different and we all need to understand what it means to us as individuals rather than follow a 'happiness formula' in the hope that we'll suddenly get it.

I am always happy when I feel like I have a purpose and am living out that purpose in the best way I can. For others, happiness is more of a sensory experience, the thrill of stepping off a plane in a new country, for example. (I have to admit, that makes me happy too.)

SELF-ACTUALIZATION
Pursue Inner Talent
Creativity   Fulfilment

SELF-ESTEEM
Achievement   Mastery
Recognition   Respect

BELONGING – LOVE
Friends   Family   Spouse   Lover

SAFETY
Security   Stability   Freedom from Fear

PHYSIOLOGICAL
Food   Water   Shelter   Warmth

Wifi

For you, it might be the feeling of being connected with the world and with the people around you. Or time to create something meaningful. Either way, when you feel happy, you feel free in your choices, confident in yourself, grateful for all the good things in your life and energized (rather than pressured) to keep making improvements.

Happiness is clearly subjective to a large degree, but the research gives us a big clue that once you have a roof over your head and food on the table, it's the experiences you enjoy and the relationships you nourish during life that bring the most enjoyment. The Grant Study, which followed hundreds of male undergraduate students over seventy-five years, was interested in the factors that most contributed to 'human flourishing' and discovered that one of the strongest positive correlations related to the perception of flourishing was between the warmth of relationships and your health and happiness.

Dr Dan Siegel created the 'Healthy Mind Platter' to illustrate that there are a number of areas we need to encourage if we are to look after our mind and our wellbeing. These areas are:

▶ sleep

▶ physical activity

▶ focus

▶ time for reflection

▶ relaxation

▶ play

▶ connection

If we were to nurture each of these areas of life just a little then it might become both simpler and sweeter. If, however, our life is all work and no play we soon start to burn out, our productivity struggles despite (in fact, because of) all the hours we're putting in. If we have no time for reflection then we tend to carry on blindly, often saying yes to things that in our heart of hearts we don't want to do but feel we 'should'. And if we don't look after our body through good sleep and physical exercise, our energy nosedives: our engine might be running, but we have the wrong fuel in the tank.

The recipe for optimum happiness and wellbeing is different for each of us, but it's up to you to choose how you live your life and use the ingredients that are to hand. You know deep down what satisfies your hunger. If you can't imagine being able to 'fit in' all of these elements in your life as it is right now, then you need to be willing to make changes.

Happiness leads to success

Scientists agree that happiness matters; the happier you are, the more likely you are to be successful, healthy and live a long life. I think most of us are conditioned to believe that happiness results from success, but in fact it's the other way round: it's the people who make themselves happy by prioritizing the tasks they enjoy and the people they love who are often the most successful.

If you sacrifice or defer your happiness in the quest for success, you're doing yourself a huge disservice. The point is well made by Shawn Achor, author of *The Happiness Advantage*. If you do what you love, if you give yourself the time to figure out what you love and what you really want, then you are more likely to be successful. When you instinctively feel that what you are doing with your life matters, and you eliminate the elements that are unhelpful or negative, you become more productive by doing less, but doing what's important. So, as Steve Jobs said, if you haven't found it yet, don't settle. Keep writing down your ideas, keep exploring and notice what brings you happiness and a sense of fulfilment.

It's the same with relationships; the people in your life who bring out good feelings in you, who encourage you to be courageous, confident and happy, are the people you will always go out of your way to help in any way you can. People who make us happy bring out our best.

Happiness isn't a consequence of living a successful life; success is the consequence of living a happy life.

Create the perfect blend

For many of us, 'work' and 'life' are no longer two separate things that we put on opposite sides of a scale, weighing one against the other and doing our best to find a balance. Through technology, it's increasingly difficult to separate time at work from time at home. The upside is that many people now have more flexible working hours: we can conduct our meetings using Skype and catch up on projects away from the distractions and interruptions of a busy office. The downside is that, now the lines between work and life are so blurred, it's becoming that much more important to create a work–life blend that works for us. For me, that means waking up at 5 a.m. and working in a super-productive state for three hours, then running with my son to school through the park, followed by a mix of creative time and 'doing' time. I make sure I reserve at least one day a week for face-to-face meetings with people who can make a real difference to me and my business.

Harvard Business School conducted interviews with almost 4,000 executives worldwide and discovered that effective business leaders often had in common the ability to carefully combine their work with their family and community life. They make *deliberate choices* about what to agree to and what to decline, rather than engage in constant firefighting, because they understand that time is limited and so they need to keep hold of what matters as their career develops.

These leaders tend to involve their loved ones both in what they do and in making important decisions. They know what success looks like to them personally, and devote time and energy to building their support networks. We might think we need to prove ourselves as individuals, but the key to our success is in collaboration and managing our own human resources or 'capital'. In that way, the sum of our life is greater than the individual parts. Instead of trying to keep everything separate, and in doing so spending too much time and energy running between the different areas of our life, trying to juggle them all at once, we should bring them together in order to prioritize what really matters.

5. THE 80:20 LIFE

The Pareto Principle is a well-documented statistical tool. It is based on an observation by Italian economist Vilfredo Pareto in 1906 that 80 per cent of income in Italy was received by 20 per cent of the population. The ratio was subsequently found to apply in many other fields, and is one we can use here to good effect. In businesses, for example, often around 80 per cent of an organization's profit will be generated by just 20 per cent of its customers.

I use the principle myself, and often remind myself to focus on the most valuable 20 per cent of my business activities, but far more than that, the 80:20 principle helps me to prioritize in just about every area of my life. Whether it's productivity, profit, passions or people – when you prioritize the few things that really matter you bring more happiness, love and success into life.

I use 80:20 to help me focus on gaining strength and expertise in the most important areas, instead of attempting to improve every weakness. It even helps me to maintain a healthy lifestyle: rather than trying to be good 100 per cent of the time, I begin by focusing on the healthy things I love, like my morning run and eating a delicious, healthy breakfast. That 20 per cent of my day has a positive effect on the rest of it, absolving me from the pressure to be perfect for the remaining 80 per cent (and for the inevitable failure to do so).

If you over-extend yourself, there will come a time when something has to give. Don't let that be your health, your sanity or your relationships. When the spinning plates begin to wobble, apply the 80:20 principle and let those you don't need fall to the ground. Each morning you should prioritize what you're going to do for the rest of the day. That's really difficult if you feel that every task is of equal importance. Simplify it by asking yourself what is the one thing you can do today that will make the biggest difference. Start with that, and your most important 20 per cent will soon take shape.

In Part Four there are a number of productivity tools based on the 'less is more' philosophy. They enable you to achieve more in less time, by prioritizing what's important, chunking down large goals into more practical steps and scheduling your time efficiently.

You don't need to be good at everything. Why not be world class at one thing instead?

In the next chapter you're going to focus in on your strengths. So many of us are conditioned to believe that we always need to be working on our weak points so that we can be good at everything. Do we wonder if a concert pianist is good at doing her own bookkeeping, or whether Richard Branson is a dab hand with a paintbrush? Focus on what you do best; if you're in sales, be the best sales person in the company, and even if you're in charge of a small company and you need to cover a few different roles, grow by feeding your strengths and prune back the weak branches. Trying to be all things to all people, whether in business or in your personal life, just gets you trapped on the hamster wheel.

I always ask for help when I need it. I never feel it diminishes me, in fact I think it's what helps me grow. I try to stay open to learning and accepting that there are a lot of things I still don't know. I believe asking is like a muscle, the more you exercise it, the easier it becomes to keep doing it. Asking for help is not a sign of weakness, it is a sign that you are human. No one has all the answers. We are not supposed to do everything ourselves; that is a modern-day myth that needs to be retired. It serves no good purpose, either for ourselves or others. One of our greatest sources of fulfilment comes from our sense of purpose and belonging; helping others actually makes us happy and vice versa. So, not only is it OK to ask for help, it's GOOD to ask for help!

In this chapter, however, I want you to focus on your passions and the people who matter.

What makes you feel alive?

> ❮ *Don't ask yourself what the world needs. Ask yourself what makes you come alive and then go do that. Because what the world needs is people who have come alive.* ❯
>
> Howard Thurman

Which magazines can't you walk by without picking them up and immediately thumbing through them?

Remember when you felt really good about something you were doing or achieved. Describe what it was that made you feel that way.

What themes come up in your life that you are drawn to?

What lessons or experiences would you want to share with others?

passion: an intense desire or enthusiasm for something

values: one's judgement of what is important in life

Who are your people?

❦ One day spent with someone you love can change everything. ❧

Mitch Albom, *For One More Day*

If you apply the 80:20 principle to your personal life, you will get even greater returns. Take your social circle as an example: 20 per cent of your friends will give you 80 per cent of your joy, yet we try to fit everyone in. It's impossible. We accept invitations to events we're not even sure we want to go to but we can't find a couple of hours for our closest friend who always puts a smile on our face. Far better to identify the top 20 per cent of people in your life who make you happiest, and schedule time with them first. I'm not suggesting cutting anyone out of your life, and of course not everyone we love makes us happy all the time, but you have to make sure you prioritize those who matter most to you.

Whether at home or at work, prioritizing the 20 per cent of people who make the biggest positive difference to your life will bring you many of your greatest rewards. If you focus on the people who really matter, rather than trying to be all things to all people and spreading yourself too thin, you will make a big difference to their lives too.

Trying to force connections or keeping people around us who either don't bring out our best or are just plain hard work doesn't help either them or us. Prolonging relationships, whether business or personal, that are one sided or fractious is another way that we overcomplicate our lives. Sometimes letting go is the best thing we can do. Not only do you ditch the negative, you also create more room for the positive people so that you can give them more of your time, love and attention. In return, you'll experience a lot more fun, creativity and laughter together.

❝ *When you stop doing things for fun,*
you might as well be dead. ❞
Ernest Hemingway

Nurture your support network

❝ *It's not how you get knocked down that counts,*
it's how you get back up. ❞
Traditional boxing motto

Life will always throw up unexpected situations. It's how you deal with them that counts.

If you want to do fulfilling work and live the life you want, and give both your full attention, then building a support network is essential. Sometimes you might just need to ask for help. If you have a support network, then when life knocks you down you can *always* get back up.

My support network is my greatest gift. You might think that asking for help will make you feel vulnerable, but really it is a great strength, because the more you feel supported in life the more you can in turn help and support others.

I find it easy to ask for help, but I still have limiting beliefs that can hold me back. The problem is they disguise themselves so well that sometimes they are impossible to see.

Once again, quality is a great deal more valuable than quantity when it comes to your support network, whether personally or professionally. Focusing on my professional network, for example, has enabled me to connect with the very best people for particular projects, and on a personal level my small group of friends have picked me up off the floor during the most painful times.

Be honest: who are the people who truly support you, and who are those who aren't so helpful to have around? I'm not arguing you should surround yourself with sycophants, but listen carefully to your instincts and prioritize those who are genuinely on your side, even if you don't always agree with them. Imagine your support network as your life-support machine – you don't want just anyone in charge of the switch.

If you had an emergency at 3 a.m. in a foreign country, who could you call to be there for you? They're the people you need in your support network.

How does your support network look right now?

Who do you already turn to for advice? Having different points of view from people you trust and care about can be really helpful as you make the tough decisions.

Many outwardly successful people have done well to get so far and be so strong without help. But if they *did* spend some time developing their support network they might be able to relax occasionally, do a little less and lean on others a little more. After all, they would do the same if a friend or colleague needed their assistance.

Say, for example, you are juggling being a parent with starting up or running your own business. You might be running yourself ragged dropping off and picking up your children from school, after-school clubs, sleepovers, weekend sport, you name it. There might be three other parents in the same situation who would jump at the chance of sharing the rides, and at the same time you have created an immediate four-person support network.

Alternatively, you might have a support network already pretty well formed, but need to practise asking for help. Don't feel bad about this; so long as you're prepared to reciprocate then you're never just taking but giving and offering, too.

In the business world, creating a network of supporters will carry you further than you could have dreamed if you'd been going it alone. How do most sales or deals start? Because you or your product came highly recommended. If you take the time to develop a few quality connections, then when the time comes that you need help or a recommendation yourself, the confidence you have gained through building and nurturing those connections will enable you to ask.

❝ *If you want to go fast . . . go alone. If you want to go far . . . go together.* ❞

African proverb

The 'less is more' route to happiness

Set fewer but more meaningful goals.

Focus on just your own progress, rather than comparing with others.

Appreciate small moments in your day.

Be grateful for what you have in your life.

When you start to focus on the parts of your life and the people who inspire and energize you, you remind yourself of all the good things you already have, rather than constantly being on the search for *more*. More 'stuff' is just a temporary fix; genuine abundance starts with gratitude. If you can take a few minutes each day to remind yourself of all the things in your life you are grateful for, all the opportunities and exciting choices you have, you automatically begin to focus your life on the things and people that make you happy and bring success. Stop comparing yourself to others and worrying about the things you don't have – focus on what's good and how you can prioritize more of these things and people in your life.

I believe that being happy *and* successful are interdependent. Once you start doing less of 'everything' and more of what you love, your happiness will come through your actions every day. Those who thrive make time for what's important to them. They are fully aware of who and what brings out their happiness, so they prioritize these people and things. They have clear goals and a path to achieve them, but equally they know it won't all be plain sailing. They embrace fear and have no time for regret.

< EXERCISE >

WHAT MAKES YOU HAPPY?

Write a list of all the things that make you the most happy –
I mean that deliver the top 20 per cent of your happiness.
Here's mine for some ideas:

- Travelling.
- Live music.
- My house filled with laughter and people I love.
- Learning something new.
- Great food.

Now think of the people who make you the happiest. If
you're lucky, you will have lots of people who make you
happy, but there will be the special ones, the ones who
always energize you, who are there through thick and
thin . . . the ones who, when you're in their company, the
days seem brighter. Now look at the first list – which of
those things do they like to do? Now pick up the phone and
get scheduling! If Ben loves live music, then go and book
concert tickets. If Jo loves travelling, plan a short weekend
away together.

Personally, just to invite all the people I love over for
Sunday lunch once a month increases my happiness tenfold!

6. OWN YOUR POWER

When we are feeling overwhelmed by all the things we think we should be doing, we need to take a step back and evaluate. Are we really the best person for all these tasks, or are we indulging our inner control freak? Yes, we all like to believe we are indispensable, or that we can do the accounts while driving the kids to their after-school clubs and then write three brilliant blogs in the evening while preparing a keynote speech. We're kidding ourselves.

The sooner we begin to focus on our real strengths and passions rather than trying to be all things to all people, the sooner we improve at what we do – and become happier while we're doing it.

strength: a good or beneficial quality or attribute of a person or thing

According to the Gallup Strengths Center website (www.gallupstrengthscenter.com), people who use their strengths every day are six times more likely to be engaged in their work. When you focus on doing more of the things you are good at, rather than trying to do everything, you find yourself in the 'flow', as Mihaly Csikszentmihalyi famously termed it, that feeling of being immersed in what you are doing. Flow means:

▶ increased energy and engagement
▶ an ability to learn more rapidly
▶ higher performance levels
▶ being motivated to do more

Being in the state of flow not only feels good, it's where we perform at our peak. We are truly in our element. If you want to create your best work you need to enjoy it while challenging and using your best skills. When you are focused on what you're doing right in the moment, you pay attention to the details and are more likely to come up with solutions. If you're constantly being distracted by too many equally urgent but less important tasks, you'll struggle ever to get into the flow. This is when we feel that we are busy all day long but achieving little.

It's easy to tell when I'm in the flow: everything becomes simple. It's not that work magically gets done for me, but it seems to get done at twice the pace with half the effort. When I'm in the flow, my best work is created, the work that gets results. It's when I lose track of time and, while I might feel challenged by the task in hand, I never feel overwhelmed by it. It's the intersection between my strengths, my skills, my passions and my work.

< EXERCISE >

ARE YOU SELLING YOURSELF SHORT?

List five strengths/assets you have:

1.

2.

3.

4.

5.

Some suggestions: creativity / communication / empathy /
leadership / humour / optimism / sense of adventure /
attention to detail / loyalty / modesty / discipline /
prudence / intuition / sense of appreciation / forgiving /
fairness / kind / loving / energetic / persistence / curious /
open-mindedness / student / teacher.

The full interactive 'Strengths and Passions'
questionnaire can be found online at www.shaa.com/
passions

How effectively do you use your strengths in your everyday life? Write down a concrete example against each strength of when you last made good use of it. Which of these attributes, when you are putting them into use, makes you feel like your true, authentic self? Your strengths are a great indicator of what motivates you to get up on a wet morning in February; if you're not putting them to good use then your performance levels will suffer.

If you know your strengths, then you can approach problems or difficult situations aware of the tools you have to hand. If you procrastinate when faced by something that requires attention to detail, such as filling in a weekly spreadsheet, and you realize you have no 'attention to detail' skill but you have 'communication' skill in abundance, why not use your powers of persuasion to outsource or delegate the task? In return, you might offer to help with something they're having trouble with but which plays to your strengths.

Integrate your strengths more in what you do, begin to really own them, talk about them with others and share ideas about how to use them in the various areas of your life. You know when you are using your strengths well because you have an abundance of that feel-good energy, you're happy to work hard and put the effort in. You're connected and doing what feels right.

No doubt at some point in your life you have been told not to show off. It's vulgar, it's rude, it's a sign of an inflated ego. But knowing your strengths is not showing off: it's the key to doing more with less effort. Focusing only on work that plays to your strengths is the key to happiness.

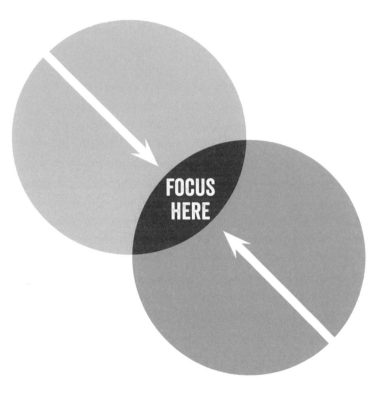

PASSIONS

FOCUS
HERE

STRENGTHS

Understanding and acknowledging your weaker areas shouldn't be dismissed – it's important to know the areas in which you need to ask for help. But know your strengths first, because they are the best things you have to build on, and the best things you have to offer in exchange for help from others.

When you combine your passions and what brings you happiness with what you're good at, then things really start to improve; in fact, they become amazing. You start to live the life you were supposed to live. So think how you might bring more of you and what makes you tick into what you do, rather than trying to be all things to all people.

Doing less of what you're not so great at and concentrating instead on what you are good at sets up a virtuous cycle of productivity, with the bonus of extra happiness thrown in. I'm not suggesting you ignore your weaknesses, but stop letting them take up all your time while draining your confidence.

You don't have to do everything yourself.

< EXERCISE >

WHERE DOES YOUR POWER
COME FROM?

➡ What motivates you to succeed?

➡ What do you feel most passionate about?

➡ What are you really good at?

➡ When do you most feel like you are on purpose?

➡ If you knew you couldn't fail, what would you do?

PART THREE:
A 'LESS IS MORE' LIFE

❛ The key is not to prioritize what's on your schedule, but to schedule your priorities. ❜

Stephen Covey

I realize I've already stated this, but I can't stress enough how important it is to align what you do with your values, strengths and passions. When we do what we love it's so much easier to *keep* doing it.

I can be physically exhausted from juggling an overseas work trip with writing a presentation for a speaking engagement and helping my son with his homework. But, because I love doing all these things, I have the mental energy and motivation to do them. Of course, I need to take time to recharge my batteries like everyone else, but when we are forced to do things that don't even make us happy then we become drained and depleted much faster. I can guarantee you I would be a whole lot more exhausted if I were juggling spreadsheets, employment contracts and updating a project management plan. Fortunately there are people who *love* doing those things for me – and typically they hate doing the stuff I love.

If we build upon areas where we are already strong, we develop our strengths and therefore our resilience when it comes to more challenging times. The alternative is that we spend our lives trying to fix what is wrong, stubbornly insisting 'I can do it' while missing out on all the things we do really well with joy and ease. You can put up your hand and ask for help with all the other things; they'll get done much more quickly that way, too.

Building on our strengths doesn't mean that we never

101

venture out into the unknown. It's just that we learn to approach new situations and challenges with our own personality and attributes, rather than blindly trying to follow a set of rules that don't seem to fit very well for us. It is when we are happy that we think more clearly, are creative, come up with ideas and make quicker, more confident decisions.

Being happy is the best route to getting more done. As soon as we begin to suffer in work or any area of life, our productivity nosedives.

♥

REMIND YOURSELF OF WHAT GETS YOU
UP IN THE MORNING. DO LESS OF EVERYTHING ELSE AND
MORE OF THAT, STARTING TODAY.

IF YOU REALLY WANT TO DO SOMETHING, DON'T GIVE YOURSELF
ANY ALTERNATIVE. IF LIFE DEPENDS ON IT, PLAN A HAS TO WORK.
YOU MIGHT NEED TO TWEAK OR PIVOT, BUT STAY IN THE GAME.

WHO NEEDS TWO PLANS? WE ONLY HAVE ONE LIFE.

DON'T PUT YOUR HOPES AND DREAMS INTO PLAN B – IF DOING
SOMETHING IS THE RIGHT THING, MAKE PLAN A WORK.

LIFE ISN'T A REHEARSAL, SO DON'T HIDE
YOUR DREAMS UNDER THE BED.

TODAY IS THE DAY TO COMMIT TO PLAN A.

♥

7. YOUR INSTINCT IS RIGHT, THE SYSTEM IS WRONG

❬ Trust instinct to the end, even though you can give no reason. ❭

Ralph Waldo Emerson

Worrying about stuff takes up so much time and gets in the way of getting on with the things we'd love to do, or at least start. We need the confidence to put all the 'what ifs' aside and make quicker, simpler decisions without constantly worrying about the outcome, because none of us can ever be entirely certain what will or won't happen.

Trust goes hand-in-hand with confidence, the confidence to trust yourself and trust others. The confidence to filter out what isn't working for you and say no more often, giving you room to say yes to more of the right things at the right time. It's using all your past knowledge and experience in combination with your instincts and your intuition to stop constantly questioning and worrying and start doing.

When we have confidence, we are less likely to get stuck in the trap of analysis paralysis; we give things a go knowing that whatever happens, inside we'll still be OK. When you feel OK about yourself as a person, you have a strength that allows you to let go of fear and excuses more easily. You spend less time beating yourself up and more time getting on with it.

confidence: the feeling or belief that one can have faith in or rely on someone or something

self-confidence: a feeling of self-assurance arising from an appreciation of one's own abilities or qualities

Our early life usually determines whether we are naturally self-confident, but a happy, easy childhood doesn't necessarily guarantee confidence as an adult: often it is the knowledge that we have made it through challenges and problems that makes us believe we can do so again.

Confidence means that we know and understand ourselves and our abilities. It means we are able to trust in the abilities of others, rather than thinking we have to do it all by ourselves. It means we are comfortable in our own skin and feel optimistic about our plans and the future, even when we know we have no guarantee about the outcomes. True confidence means that we embrace our vulnerabilities and flaws but go ahead and give everything our best shot anyway.

Too many people waste their lives worrying about their 'labels' – too old, too young, too fat or from the wrong school or neighbourhood. We create a million excuses for ourselves. We all do it, but that doesn't make it right or helpful. There's nothing to stop you from writing a new story. I know this from personal experience: it's the only way out of the trap that we create for ourselves.

Less is more even when it comes to confidence. It is better for confidence to be authentic and compassionate than to be overblown and full of ego and pride. You don't need to be the loudest person in the room to feel confident in yourself. Arrogance will only build a barrier between you and your true instincts.

Confidence is the ability to filter out the interference and know what feels right in your heart. And not only know it, but follow it.

Never be afraid to try

Trusting your instincts might feel like the scary option at first. You worry that you'll feel like a failure if things don't work out. But I don't know anyone who regretted trying. There's something about following your heart that gives you a strength, even when things don't go according to the plan. You gave it your best shot, you can't ask for more than that. You begin to notice that even when the plan doesn't turn out quite how you imagined, it's just as good a journey.

The human capacity for finding the silver lining to almost any cloud is quite incredible. I know many successful business people who encountered potentially catastrophic setbacks along the way that became their biggest lessons and their most valuable gifts. Even something as serious as bankruptcy can be a blessing in disguise. There are financial institutions that would prefer to lend to someone who has already gone bankrupt once, as they have less chance of doing so ever again.

Everyone can have inner confidence, often we just need to find the key to unlock it

Nurture the things that already bring out the confident side of you and use the skills you already have to address how to be more confident in other areas. For example, if you are good at talking to people one-on-one but struggle with speaking in public or on camera, begin to treat the audience as a single person. The best presentations, whether live or on screen, are those where you feel that the presenter is simply having a conversation with you. Make a connection with your words and with that 'one person', be yourself, smile as you would smile in a conversation, and enjoy the feeling of the connection you are making.

Turn up your inner voice

In a real crisis we hear our intuition come through loud and clear. We have no time for indecision; suddenly, simply, we just seem to know what to do.

On a day-to-day basis it isn't so easy to keep our minds calm and clear of chatter; we might tend to overanalyse every situation to the point of never making a decision, have so

many ideas that we don't know which to action or we let fearful, negative thinking take over.

Sports psychologist Dr Steve Peters calls this the 'chimp' or emotional mind that can overwhelm the human mind if we let it constantly run riot. The chimp mind can be very noisy, chattering away, and therefore we need to calm ourselves if we're going to be able to hear our inner, human voice.

When I need to clear my mind I will take a day or two and go to the countryside or coast, switch everything off and gradually let things calm down. My daily run helps as well:

it makes me breathe deeply and the effort helps to release tension in my mind.

For others, daily meditation, even for a few minutes, gives the mind a chance to rest and reboot. (I have to admit I am still struggling to get to grips with meditation, but I haven't given up. The one time I can meditate is when I'm swimming. The repetitive nature of going up and down and the 'white noise' of the water means there is nothing to distract me; it is the perfect environment to help calm the chimp and reconnect with my inner voice.)

> ❦ *If you try to calm it [the mind], it only makes it worse, but over time it does calm, and when it does, there's room to hear more subtle things – that's when your intuition starts to blossom and you start to see things more clearly and be in the present more.* ❧
>
> Steve Jobs

Trust in others

The quality rather than the quantity of your relationships will also help to build your inner confidence, because you can put your trust in quality relationships.

Like so many good things in life, the best way to get trust is to give it – that is my philosophy about pretty much everything. When we have trust, we have openness and honesty. It allows you to move on more quickly when problems do arise because you are much less interested in playing the blame game.

To gain the trust of others, the easiest thing is to lead by example. For instance, when you mess up, admit it immediately rather than pretend it never happened. If you have an attitude of openness and humility, people will come to your aid when you need help; they'll offer solutions rather than standing on the sidelines.

The ability to ask for help, and simply to know it is there if you should ever need it, is a sign of true inner confidence. Like most things, just by doing it you begin to build that confidence as you see people respond to your requests.

Small acts of confidence

Confidence is like a muscle that can be developed over time. If you learn to act differently, you'll start to think differently too. There have been many studies showing that if you act 'as if' through your conscious choice of words and body language, you begin to change how you think and feel. It's not quite 'fake it till you make it', but there's something to be said for the general principle.

Amy Cuddy, social psychologist and associate professor at Harvard Business School, noticed that although the men and women who entered the MBA programme were all of equal academic ability, the men would on average gain better results. Cuddy wanted to understand why this was happening and discovered that it was because the MBA was graded on 50 per cent participation – men were doing better because they were more assertive in class.

Cuddy decided to teach the less naturally assertive

students techniques in confident body language; as a result their actual confidence improved and their grades shot up. Clearly, a lack of confidence in class could have a significant impact on someone's future career, since those with the best grades typically get the best offers. Even more galling then to admit that you knew all the answers but were too afraid to raise your hand. Cuddy's intervention thus had an impact not just on the students' grades, but potentially on their future careers too.

You don't need to be confident about everything. No one is. It's much easier to be really good at, and therefore confident about, things that combine your strengths and passions.

For example, you would like to ask for a raise or a promotion at work but you don't feel confident enough to do so. Remind yourself of all the qualities and abilities that you bring to your job, focus on the key areas where you deliver real results, rather than the whole job description; write them down. Now you have concrete evidence, you can begin to really appreciate what you do, which will increase your confidence when talking to your boss.

Look at the times when you feel more confident and do those activities more often. It may sound obvious but sometimes it is as though we forget about all the things we are good at and get mired in negative feelings caused by a situation in which we lacked confidence.

Think about children who lack confidence in their academic ability but then discover a talent in music or sport. When that talent is nurtured by a great teacher and encouraged, then a child's confidence flourishes, and once this happens, their academic grades tend to go up too. It's the same in the workplace or in our relationships. We all bring individual strengths and talents to the mix.

Once you stop worrying about what everyone else thinks of you, or whether you are good enough to be sitting at the table, then you will begin to unleash your true potential.

< EXERCISE >
ACT 'AS IF' . . .

Imagine now how it would feel to be confident: would you act differently, what are the kinds of things you would say? How would your body language look?

Want to be fitter and healthier? Act as if you already are. What would the super healthy you choose for breakfast? Ever watch a reality-TV diet show? There's a reason they treat the contestants like athletes and not couch potatoes; they want them to become like athletes.

Want to be the 'go to' expert in your field? Draw on all your experience and start being the best, adding to your skills and knowledge all the time. Read books, go to seminars, workshops, dial in to webinars. There is a plethora of ways to gain extra knowledge; you no longer have to be tied to a desk to learn or improve a skill.

Want a promotion at work? Step up to the responsibility right now, show that you have what it takes. Start acting as if you were already doing the job.

Book a course, networking event, seminar or talk today that you're really interested in attending. Interacting with like-minded people not only creates more connections, but boosts your confidence, especially if you make it a regular thing. Every year I look forward to my friend Jayson Gaignard's Mastermind Talks where he brings together like-minded individuals in an intimate setting. I always leave more connected, equipped, inspired and committed to leading the life I desire.

As I know from first-hand experience (see p. 197), one single event or conference can change your life.

8. EDIT, FILTER, FOCUS

We want to please people, we want people to like us, we want to feel included and needed. So when they ask us for a meeting, we say yes; when they ask if we can help, we say yes; when they ask us for a coffee, we say yes; and when they say 'Would you *just* . . . ?' we just say . . . 'Yes'.

Every time we say yes to something we aren't really engaged with, that we don't really want to do, we are taking time away from saying yes to the things and people we love. There are only twenty-four hours in the day and by the time you've finished procrastinating, commuting, checking emails and daily life, not to mention sleeping, you won't have many left to be productive.

Think carefully about how and with whom you want to spend those hours.

Do you find it hard to say no? Are you trying to be all things to all people, even when you know it's impossible and means you'll do nothing well? Learning to focus on what's important, and ignore what's unimportant, is critical if you want to get more of what matters done. Once you can begin to master this, and there are a number of ways you can practise, you will feel more in control of your own time, you'll be able to see things through to the finish rather than starting so many projects with so many people that you end up running from one to another, leaving them all half-done, waiting for your return.

To truly master this skill, I highly recommend reading James and Claudia Altucher's excellent book, *The Power of No*.

Signs that you are saying yes when you really need to say no

You avoid speaking your mind.
You find it hard to express a difference of opinion.
You consistently put everyone else's needs above your own.
You wouldn't mind if someone else just took over and told you what to do.
You can find it hard to know exactly what you want.
You worry what people will think of you if you say no.
You feel guilty when you say no, even when it's something you really don't want to do.

If you are a 'people pleaser' it isn't all bad – because once you really begin to channel those attributes of generosity and service in the right direction you'll be making a lot of people happy. You just need to stop trying to please all of the people, all of the time, and instead pick your beneficiaries and your projects. When you constantly put others' needs above your own, too often you will begin to neglect yourself. You may neglect your healthy lifestyle, or you might neglect your mental health and begin to feel stressed.

A balance is essential – if you take better care of yourself then you will feel stronger and more energized to take better care of others. Too much stress leads to a decrease in performance, so as you take on more tasks, you become less efficient and even more stressed out. This is when we can really start to lose our sense of enjoyment of life, whether in our job, in our relationships or both. It all feels like too much and we're not sure how to get things back on track. Not only that, but everyone else seems quite happy to keep loading us up with new requests, even when they say to us they are worried we're taking on too much. This can lead to a build-up of frustration and/or resentment that can explode in sudden anger. Even worse, if you keep it suppressed it will eat away at your self-esteem.

This is the time to set some *boundaries*. To do that, you need to identify what motivates you to agree to something that goes against all your instincts. Why do you say yes in such situations? Is it that you are afraid of the reaction if you say no? Most people in these circumstances fear either rejection or being seen as a failure and less than perfect. These may be deep-rooted patterns that began early in life, and may even need professional help to overcome. If so, don't be afraid to seek it.

There are also practical ways you can set boundaries that will help you say yes to what's important and say no without fear or guilt. Or perhaps you have simply got into a habit of saying yes all the time. It's an easy habit to acquire when you are working your way up the career ladder – how can you say no to your boss and look good? But if you say yes rather than explaining that you are already working on a task with a set deadline, the quality of your work will inevitably suffer. It's much better to say sooner rather than later that you have other commitments; then you can work out together which to prioritize.

How to say no without feeling bad

It can be hard to say no, but here are some ways to make it easier. Sometimes you want to say 'no', sometimes you want to say 'no, not right now' and sometimes you might want to say 'maybe'.

I'm sorry, but I can't commit to this right now.

Let me think about it and I'll get back to you. Note: This is more like a maybe, but buys you time if you're not sure if you want to do it or have the time to do it.

I don't think I'm the best person to help you, but perhaps you could try . . . [suggest someone else]

I can't do it right now, but I could schedule some time . . . [suggest a date]

I can't do this, but I can . . . [suggest an alternative]

I'm sorry, as much as I'd like to, I just don't have the time.

I'd love to do this, but I can't because . . . [give a good reason]

Sorry, this isn't something I'm able to do.

If the request is something more simple, such as meeting for a coffee, you can still say no firmly, but politely. Honesty is always the best policy. The most important thing to remember is that whenever you say no to something you don't want to do, or don't have the time to do, you're making room to say yes to something you really do want to do.

< EXERCISE >

NO IS A COMPLETE SENTENCE

List five things you've agreed to do, but really wish you'd said no.

1.

2.

3.

4.

5.

Now list five reasons why you said yes, when you really wanted to say no.

1.

2.

3.

4.

5.

When your instincts tell you that you're saying yes too often, LISTEN to them.

When you are asked to do something, question its *relevance* – for example, is it relevant to the core of your job/your development or is it just someone trying to offload it? If you're not wasting your time with irrelevant tasks then you have more time to be really effective and helpful, you can make more of a positive difference to the work and people that really matter.

Practise saying no to small things. You need to see that the world won't end if you say no, that the reality is that if you tried to do everything that you were ever asked, you'd just end up stretching yourself and feeling guilty that you weren't doing anything well.

If you're not sure whether to say yes or no, instead of instantly saying yes just in case, try buying yourself some time – 'Thank you, let me see if that fits in with everything else I have to do and I'll get back to you.' Or, 'My current tasks are x, y and z. Which would you like me to delay in order to do this one?'

It's the same if you are starting a new business – don't try to be all things to all people, but instead really narrow down your focus. What's your niche? What is the *one* specific problem/desire that your product or service provides a solution for? What are you an *expert* in?

You need to live life for you, not just for everyone else, or you might keep running, working all hours of the day and night, trying to be everything to everyone and somehow feeling that things will never quite fall into place. Would you let your best friend run themselves into the ground? Listen to your heart and act on your own best advice. Resolve to let go of *everything* that isn't making your life better, sweeter or richer so that you can make room for everything that does.

I know this isn't easy. This isn't a natural thing. You are re-engineering everything you have been conditioned to believe. You don't need to do more to get more.

< EXERCISE >
YES/NO CHECKLIST

List five things you've agreed to do, but really wish
you'd said no.

SAY YES IF:	SAY NO IF:
it needs to be done	its purpose is unclear
it's worth doing	it's not going to benefit either of you in the long run
you are capable	someone else could do it equally well or better
you want to	your motivation to say yes is fear – of how you might look, what they might say, whether they will be upset or offended
your head and heart agree	your head and/or heart disagree

If you could only say yes to 20 per cent of the things that you
were asked, which would be the most important / bring the
most joy / be most effective?

Filter

> ❝ *If you chase two rabbits, both will escape.* ❞
>
> Native American saying

If you want to begin to change the pattern, to allow space for those really important things to get to the front of the queue, the most effective way is to concentrate on **one goal at a time** rather than trying to tackle three simultaneously. Whether it's an idea for a new way of doing something at work, focusing all your efforts on seeing through a single project you believe in, giving your family more of your attention or making a lifestyle change, you need to commit to ONE thing at a time. Or at least one thing in each area.

The more choices we give ourselves, the harder it becomes to choose, like taking a seat in an almost empty theatre. The American Society for the Prevention of Cruelty to Animals tested the 'less is more' theory by reducing the number of cats on show in their adoption centre in Colorado. With 40 per cent fewer cats for visitors to choose from, the adoption rate *doubled*.

Psychologist Barry Schwartz, author of *The Paradox of Choice*, found that the vast choice on offer to consumers often leads to anxiety and results in no purchase at all, so far from increasing purchases it actually has the opposite effect. The 'Jam Test', part of a study on choice by Sheena Iyengar and Mark Lepper, showed that consumers were much more likely to make a purchase when given a choice of six jams versus a choice of twenty or more, and once they'd made the choice report higher levels of satisfaction.

It's the same with speed dating: researchers discovered that a larger than average pool of potential dates available in one evening doesn't make it any easier to get asked out on one. We're all worried that 'something better' might be round the corner or that we'll make a bad choice.

How do I choose?

You might have ten great ideas that could all work out well. The problem is that if you try and follow all ten simultaneously, you might struggle to do even one of those really well; in effect you'll have wasted ten great ideas. Be brave and be willing to narrow down your ideas so that you can begin to focus your efforts on one and see it through to fruition. You might well follow up on all your ideas in time, especially if they work together within your business or life, but focus on one at a time and you're much more likely to get the results you want.

I once gave a webinar on how to use content online to leverage your business, and a business owner from Ireland asked how she could use content as a way to build up trust and relationships with her suppliers, not just her customers. She had so many ideas that she didn't know where to start, and as a result hadn't done anything about it for months. After just five minutes of thrashing it out, she had one, really strong idea – do a short weekly newsletter with a deal of the week, a case study and a tip. 'It's so obvious, I can't believe I haven't been doing it already,' she said. But it's easy to ignore the obvious when we've got too many ideas on our plate.

The first step is get all that tumble of thoughts and ideas

down on paper, so that you can begin to sort and make sense of them.

Thoughts circle like a merry-go-round with no order and little sense of priority. Trivial ideas will take up just as much space as important ones unless you are able to look at them and see them for what they are. When you actively take those ideas out of your head you can create a structure, and that's when a sense of clarity and knowing what you need to do next is more likely to come.

Personally, I love using big, differently coloured Post-it notes when I have an idea I need to make sense of or create an action plan for making something happen. The first thing I do is cover my entire wall with ideas. Just 'dump' all the ideas you have in your head on to paper. The beauty of Post-its is simply that you can move them around, as your thoughts are unlikely to surface in the perfect order. The fact that they come in all shapes, sizes and colours makes this technique even more appealing.

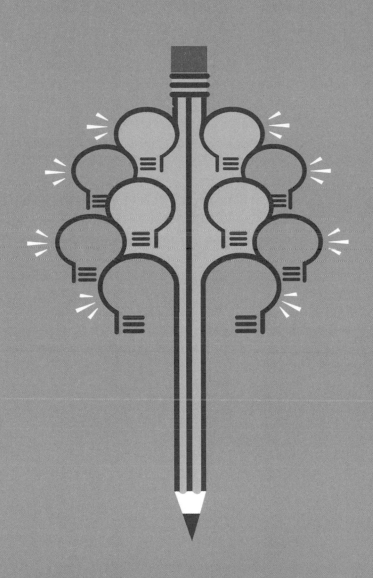

Good ideas go viral

The stats say it all – Monday is the day all health breaks loose. Every Monday, searches for health-related topics spike on Google. Every Monday is a chance for a fresh start and you get fifty-two chances in a year to get back on track if the rest of the week doesn't go so well. Here are three simple but great ideas that have taken off in a big way:

1. The Johns Hopkins Center for a Livable Future is a meeting of marketing and public health and it is where the idea for Meatless Mondays began. Sid Lerner was an advertising executive turned health advocate and launched Meatless Mondays with the JHCLF in 2003. He simply, but brilliantly, made an easy goal out of the statistic that people were more responsive to health messages on Mondays. Throw in a handy bit of memorable alliteration, and suddenly a boring message about eating more vegetables became a global phenomenon about changing habits and eating less meat, not every day, just once a week.

2. *Two scientists managed to get some historically unhealthy communities in West Virginia to consume fewer saturated fats simply by running advertisements telling them to buy low-fat milk instead of whole milk. They didn't try to change everyone's whole diet – they focused on just one change in behaviour and had remarkable results.*

3. *Infection via IV lines is common in intensive care units; it is also easily preventable. Dr Peter Pronovost at Johns Hopkins devised an extremely simple checklist comprising such basics as reminding doctors to wash their hands or to sterilize the site before inserting the needle. It's estimated that this saved around 1,500 lives in Michigan hospitals over the next eighteen months, and saved around $175 million on treating prevented complications.*

For these and other great ideas, see Chip and Dan Heath's Switch: How to Change When Change Is Hard.

< EXERCISE >

IS IT IMPORTANT, OR JUST URGENT?

It's so easy to live reactively, bouncing from one thing to the next until you can barely remember what you wanted to do to begin with. By figuring out what's really important, you can keep yourself on track even when urgent things come up.

Ask yourself:

➡ **1. What's my end goal right now?**
Don't over-think this. If you want to write a post, then the end goal is 'Write a post'. If you want to do a workout, the end goal is 'Get out the door and exercise'.

Bearing that in mind, does this task that feels urgent get you closer to that goal, or does it take you further away? The things that get you closer to your goal always take precedence over those that don't directly further your progress. By pulling out and getting a little perspective on what you really want to happen, you can step away from distracting, so-called 'urgent' tasks.

➡ **2. What are the consequences if I don't do this right now?**
I find that many people bounce like pinballs from one thing to the other – Answer emails! Answer texts! Set up appointment! Change laundry over! Answer more emails! – They're just reacting to what comes up, which totally kills

their momentum and makes it really hard to get anything meaningful done.

So when you get something coming up at you, think about the consequences of *not* getting it done. Chances are, almost everything that feels really urgent can wait until you've finished your more important tasks. Don't become dependent on the drug of urgency.

➡ 3. What's my big distraction?

Did you know that when you see a new notification on your phone, a new email, or a new message on your social media, checking that out gives you a big rush of dopamine, the same substance that is associated with many types of addiction? It's no wonder that we have so much trouble distinguishing between important and urgent!

Take a minute to think about your biggest distraction. For a long time for me, that was my phone. Though I'm much better about it now, I had to really consciously make that happen by turning off my phone when I was in meetings or at dinner with my son. What distraction will you need to consciously turn off in order to get things done?

❛ Freedom is not the absence of commitments but the ability to choose – and commit myself to – what is best for me. ❜

Paulo Coelho

Research

It's good to do your homework. For example, if you wanted to open a catering business, you might be trying to decide between a food truck or a cookery school or a beach cafe. It would be a good idea to do some research to begin to help you narrow in on 'the one'. You can research the locations that you're interested in; do any of these locations have better footfall or potential than others, are they seasonal, is there a food network you can tap into to let people know you exist or will you be working on virgin territory?

There's a big 'but' here, and that's not to get so caught up in research that it becomes an excuse not to start. I call it analysis paralysis. The purpose of research isn't to try to answer every single question about what may or may not come from the results of your decision.

Active research, also known as testing the water, can help you more than trying to be academic about it. One of the largest smoothie companies in Europe, Innocent, was founded by a group of young people who had an idea that they could make smoothies that were good for people and tasted good too. They thought this was a pretty great idea, but as they couldn't be sure they let people's taste buds help. They took a stall at a local food event and set up their smoothie machine. Then they put two barrels in front of the stall with slips of paper for people to fill out 'Yes' or 'No'. And then they asked the question, 'Should we give up our day jobs and start a smoothie company?' At the end of the day they had a barrel full of Yes votes and Innocent Smoothies was born. The company was later bought out by Coca-Cola at an estimated value of $500 million, so they were clearly doing something right.

Trust your instincts

Sometimes the act of choosing is exactly what we need to release ourselves from the never-ending weighing up of pros and cons. Sometimes it's best to give ourselves less wiggle room and follow our hearts. In his book *Essentialism*, Greg McKeown suggests that we practise putting decisions to the extreme test: if we feel 'total and utter conviction' to do something, we do it. Anything less and we say no. It sounds extreme, but I've started to apply it with resounding success.

We tend to make as many good decisions in the blink of an eye as when we weigh things up interminably, working through every possible scenario. Your instinct is based on a lot of research and living, it's not just a flippant decision. If you are willing to listen, your instincts will give you a good steer in life, just as your body will tell you what is good for your health. When you are able to filter out what's unhelpful, whether it's negative self-beliefs trying to put you off or well-intentioned but conflicting advice and opinions from others, you are able to hear what is in your heart. Making a good decision when there are too many messages coming through at the same time is really tough. With less background noise, you can listen more effectively and take quicker, more confident decisions.

When I discussed this with friends, we all agreed that when we go against our instincts we get a churning feeling in our stomachs. The older we get, the stronger the sensation becomes.

Often the true value of following our gut instinct is simply in making a decision, as opposed to being trapped in endless indecision. We never know exactly what the outcome will be, which can make it hard to just go ahead – and we will always be able to come up with a rational-sounding reason why we shouldn't pursue an idea or make a change. Sometimes we get caught up in complications of our own making, while the simplest, most obvious and often most effective choice is staring us right in the face.

You know you have made the right decision when there is peace in your heart . . . and your gut.

132

LET GO OF PERFECTION

THE KEY TO MAKING DECISIONS IS NOT TO HOLD ON
TOO TIGHTLY ONCE THEY'VE BEEN MADE.

IF IT FEELS LIKE THE WEIGHT OF THE WORLD
RESTS ON THE OUTCOME, THEN YOU NEED TO CHUNK
IT DOWN INTO SMALLER DECISIONS SO
THAT YOU CAN BE ADAPTABLE AND FLEXIBLE AS
THINGS PROGRESS.

LIFE HARDLY EVER GOES EXACTLY ACCORDING TO
PLAN: THE POINT OF A PLAN IS REALLY TO GET US
STARTED, TO MOVE US FROM THINKING OR TALKING
INTO ACTIVE DOING MODE, TO TURN OUR BIG,
VAGUE DREAMS INTO SPECIFIC TASKS THAT WE CAN
ACHIEVE BY FIXED DEADLINES.

YOU MIGHT END UP WITH AN OUTCOME DIFFERENT
FROM THE ONE YOU ORIGINALLY ENVISIONED,
AND YOU'LL HAVE GROWN AND YOU'LL HAVE
LEARNED AND DONE GREAT AND INTERESTING
THINGS ALONG THE WAY.

You can't be in control of everything, but you can choose what's important to you

There is a common trap that so many of us fall into at one time or another, and that is to try and feel in control by controlling everything around us. But this only tends to heighten our fears of being out of control and at the mercy of fate, the world, or our boss's whims. So we grip on even tighter when what we really need to do is loosen up.

None of us can predict the future with 100 per cent certainty, we can't know for sure what lies ahead, which is why we need to make the most of what we have *today*. We can't control other people or situations, and why should we? If we stop worrying about trying to force everything to fit, we can concentrate on making the most of the things that matter to us.

A little less thinking, a little more action

I'm not against thinking; thinking big, thinking through a plan, thinking of others. Yet if we're not careful then our thoughts can overwhelm us, so that we spend all our time thinking about things but never quite getting round to doing them. Sound familiar? You're in good company.

We have so many choices laid out for us every day, from where we're going to buy our lunch to which email to answer or task to get on with first, that it becomes increasingly difficult to make simple, quick decisions and increasingly easy to spend all day working hard without getting very much done. Our minds constantly whir away, just like the technology at our fingertips. Even on holiday, smartphones ensure our constant availability.

On the plus side, thanks to our high-tech world, we are in a time of creativity where start-ups are blossoming and good ideas are turning into brilliant products or services in the blink of an eye. But countless more fantastic ideas are falling by the wayside, stalled by over-thinking and over-questioning. For an idea to become reality, it needs action.

❝ *What is a good idea? One that happens is.*
If it doesn't, it isn't. ❞
Paul Arden

OVER-THINKING LEADS TO:

FEARS BECOMING SO WELL DEVELOPED WE LOSE
THE COURAGE TO START ANYTHING

PROCRASTINATION BECOMING AN OLYMPIC SPORT

TANGLED THOUGHTS OBSTRUCTING INSTINCT AND INTUITION

INCREASED CONCERN ABOUT GETTING THINGS WRONG

YOU FAILING TO FOCUS ON WHAT YOU ARE DOING BECAUSE
YOU'RE WORRYING ABOUT THINGS YOU'RE 'NOT DOING'

SAYING YES TO EVERY REQUEST FOR FEAR OF
UPSETTING OR DISPLEASING

TOO MANY OPTIONS AND TOO MUCH RESEARCH

NEVER FEELING 'READY'

TOO MANY EXCUSES NOT TO DO 'IT'

FOCUSED ACTION LEADS TO:

LIVING WITH PURPOSE

GETTING RESULTS

HAVING TIME FOR THE PEOPLE WHO MATTER

FINISHING THE PROJECTS YOU START

NOT BEING AFRAID TO CHANGE DIRECTION

TRUSTING YOUR INSTINCTS

TRUSTING OTHERS ENOUGH TO ASK FOR HELP

SHARING YOUR BEST IDEAS WITH THE WORLD

♥

9. GETTING TO THE ONE THING

By focusing on the **one thing** that you can change **right now** to make the **biggest impact**, and then mapping out the steps between where you are now and the goal you want to reach, you start to turn ideas into reality.

Ask yourself some key questions:

▶ Is this how you imagined your life to be?
▶ What's missing?
▶ Are you as healthy as you want to be?
▶ Do you love your career?
▶ How many of your dreams remain unfulfilled?
▶ What do you want?

Let's look at four areas (you can apply this process to any aspect of life, I've just picked four examples):

▶ Career
▶ Money
▶ Relationships
▶ Health

Now, pick ONE to focus on. In this area, on a scale of 1 to 10 – 1 being terrible and 10 being incredible – where are you? Why? What would need to happen to move you to an 8 and then to a 10?

Once you know what would need to happen, what ONE thing can you do about it to make it happen?

What does the one thing look like? Can you describe it clearly? Tell someone else about it: do they know what you are talking about or do they still look confused? If it's too personal, just make sure you are clear about it.

A challenge is good if it is realistic. You don't want to feel like you are putting a weight around your neck, but as if you are motivating yourself to grow. You should feel excited and, yes, perhaps a little anxious or fearful. Embrace those feelings, just like an actor about to go on stage, channel the energy. We don't grow if we don't stretch ourselves.

If you are worried that if you stop and ask yourself what you really want, you will end up with even more questions – don't panic and ignore the whole process. Instead, turn it on its head: which area of your life gets the lowest score? Start there and work your way up.

It's hard to change four things simultaneously, but if we focus on making just one positive change we will often feel the benefits more widely. For example, people who focus on changing one small eating habit, such as eating when bored, rather than immediately trying to overhaul their entire diet overnight, will be much more likely to see an improvement and break the association between eating and boredom. People who start working on freelance projects in their spare evenings are more likely to start their own business. Good habits are contagious, so once we feel the benefits of making a single change, the next change becomes a little easier.

You can get all of your life to an 8/10 and even a 10/10 if you focus on doing less but doing it better.

Mind map your ideas

Mind maps are simply a way of connecting the dots and organizing information around a core idea. They are visual, so help you see how the elements fit together; instead of a one-dimensional long list you are able to connect information in multiple directions. In your brain, ideas look like networks, with a discernible centre and lots of pathways coming off it in all directions, much like a mind map.

You can use mind mapping in a number of ways; in this instance it is an effective method to identify the actions needed to deliver an idea. Start with the thing that you want to make happen in the centre of your map. Now, around that central idea, put the actions that you need to take in order for it to happen. Some of these may need additional connectors, for example if you need a new qualification, you will need to research and apply for courses, you might need to find time in your schedule for the classes and extra income to pay for the course.

As you develop the map, you will see just what is needed for your idea to become reality, it's there in front of you rather than a vague notion in your head.

Mind mapping is an essential tool for creating more with less. It allows you to remove all the chaos and clutter in your brain. Just doing this one exercise alone will help you reap great rewards.

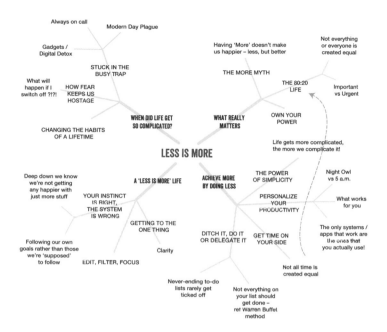

Don't wait for clarity if it isn't immediately apparent

Clarity is a wonderful thing; when you know exactly what you want and what you need to do. Clarity gives you focus and a sense of purpose; you are less distracted and you feel able to make quick decisions without all the usual confusion and worries. But if you don't feel clarity right now, don't get hung up on it. Don't *wait* for clarity.

Waiting for the green light of clarity is one of the best excuses for not getting started. Waiting for clarity can be like waiting for the perfect conditions – it's like you are waiting to be 100 per cent sure about what you're going to do, when the reality is that nothing in life is 100 per cent guaranteed; you are bound to find obstacles to negotiate and choices to make along the way.

The best route to clarity is to begin to take yourself out of the busy trap and be more present in your life from moment to moment. When you are able to focus on what you are doing or who you are with, then you'll notice the things that bring you the most joy or fulfilment – the tasks at work that combine your strengths and passions, the people you meet who inspire you. You can also begin to understand the things that hold you back or clog your day with complications; if you let go or simplify a couple of these then you'll create the space you need to develop clarity of thought and the time you need for clarity of action.

Chunk it down

Ambition is good. More than good. I've always had big goals, often the kind that make other people think I'm crazy. The reason I don't think my goals are crazy is that I chunk them down into bite-size bits. Each piece is geared towards my ideal life, but still works in my real life.

The key is not to put all your focus on the end goal, but instead on each of the steps in between. Big changes need small steps. You don't have to know what the last step is; in fact, you might not know until you get there. You just have to simplify things and get started. Once you work out how to peel back the layers on your big goals, everything becomes more achievable, whether it's running a marathon or running your own business. What's the best way to eat an elephant? One bite at a time.

Reverse engineer it

I use the image of stepping stones. You think about where you want to be, you really see it and feel it, and then you imagine a series of stepping stones coming back from your goal or idea to where you are right now. You reverse engineer it. Then you begin to map out what those stepping stones are and what you need to do to cross them.

Big ideas are great, go ahead, dream BIG, but then make sure your stepping stones are within reach of each other – what can you do *today* to take you a step closer? When you start to take your ideas out of your head and make them happen bit by bit you bring the magic to life – you get to touch it and feel it. When thinking and action go hand in hand, you become your potential.

So don't keep your big ideas hidden away in your mind, share them with the world through your actions. It doesn't even matter if an idea doesn't work out, as you can pick yourself up and get on with the next one. Far better that than pinning your hopes on an idea for years or decades only to discover it wasn't meant to be (or that someone else beat you to it).

Small victories are crucial for momentum.
If you want to achieve your goal, you have
to CHUNK IT DOWN into manageable parts.
Keep it simple — complexity just makes
things harder.

Chunk it down

Goal: Write a book

Step 1: Determine overall subject for the book

Step 2: Write the outline of the book, then outline
each chapter

Step 3: Work on one chapter at a time

Step 4: Get feedback from others

Step 5: Edit manuscript

Step 6: Send to publisher

What help do you need to make it happen?

Look at your proposed steps and your schedule. What realistically are you able to do in your timeframe and do really well? Are there tasks that you can outsource? Do you need to ask people for help to make connections or for information they might be able to offer you? Never assume you can do it all by yourself, always consider which parts of your plan might benefit from asking for help. Remember, YOU DON'T NEED TO DO EVERYTHING YOURSELF.

Make yourself accountable

When you make yourself personally accountable, you take ownership of your time, ideas and responsibilities. Being accountable requires honesty and a willingness to learn from things that go well and also how things might have been done differently.

If you can create accountability appointments with yourself and someone else, you greatly improve your chances of reaching your goal. For example, you might seek out either a mentor at work or someone you admire in your personal life. When you have to describe your goal to another person it makes you focus on being as clear as possible about what exactly you need to achieve to fulfil it. You can chunk it down into steps and check in on your progress. If you start to come up with excuses as to why you didn't stick to your plan, challenge yourself to look for a solution instead. Be honest and be willing to do things differently to get to where you want to be.

THE PROBABILITY OF ACHIEVING A GOAL

10 PER CENT IF YOU
HAVE AN IDEA

**40 PER CENT IF YOU DECIDE
YOU WILL DO IT**

**50 PER CENT IF YOU MAKE
A PLAN TO DO IT**

**65 PER CENT IF YOU PROMISE
SOMEONE ELSE YOU WILL DO IT**

95 PER CENT IF YOU HAVE
A SPECIFIC ACCOUNTABILITY
APPOINTMENT WITH THE PERSON
TO WHOM YOU COMMIT

(American Society for Training and Development; www.astd.org)

If there is an idea you want to pursue or a change you want to make, you are much more likely to see it through if you go public with it. Less is more when it comes to setting yourself very specific goals and deadlines, not just generic wishful thinking such as 'I'm going to spend more time with my family'. How *exactly* are you going to do that, what *specific* change are you going to make and how are you going to be accountable?

Schedule it

From your mind map you can now set a realistic timeline and assess what you can get done in the next week, month, three months and beyond that into the next year. You've identified the actions you need to take, the people you need to ask if you need help, and now you need to commit to the deliverables on your map. You need to get them scheduled.

Perhaps your goal is to set up a website or blog. How could you use accountability to increase the likelihood of that happening in the shortest amount of time? This is the kind of project that can go on indefinitely without a few specific goals and deadlines. Break it down into simple, achievable steps. Don't overcomplicate your ideas, your plans or your products. Simple gets done.

*When you combine getting to the ONE thing
with then doing the ONE thing, then you are a
positive force to be reckoned with.*

< EXERCISE >

HOW TO GET YOUR CAREER/WORK TO AN 8 OUT OF 10

Let's take your career. Imagine it feels like a 5 out of 10 right now and you'd like it to feel at least like an 8, but you have no idea how to make that happen. Let's focus on that area and identify one thing you can find a way to change that's going to make the biggest difference.

➡️ **What is it about your career/work that you don't like? List five things.**

1.

2.

3.

4.

5.

148

➡ **What do you like about your career/work? List five things.**

1.

2.

3.

4.

5.

➡ **What type of business or career could you pursue that will give you more of the things you love?**

➡ **Do you have the skill set, knowledge and experience needed to begin one of those careers/businesses today? If you answered yes, what are you waiting for?**

➡ **If you answered no, what do you need to do to gain the skills, knowledge or experience you need? Where can you get these? What are you waiting for?**

➡ **What could you change about your current job to improve your fulfilment rating?**

➡ **What one thing can you do before reading on that could help you on this journey? For example, can you research courses or qualifications that you'd need to change your career, then sign up for them? It is easy to get caught up in the planning stage when we try to cover every detail and eventuality. Keep it simple. Less is more.**

Ideas are nothing unless we have the courage and confidence to put them into action.

Start something today you've always wanted and you'll never regret it.

PART FOUR:
ACHIEVE MORE BY DOING LESS

❛ I think one of the things that really separates us from the higher primates is that we're tool builders. I read a study that measured the efficiency of locomotion for various species on the planet. The Condor used the least amount of energy to move a kilometre. And humans came in with a rather unimpressive showing about a third of the way down the list. It was not too proud of a showing for the crown of creation.

That didn't look so good. But then, somebody at Scientific American had the insight to test the efficiency of locomotion for a man on a bicycle. And a man on a bicycle completely blew the Condor away, completely off the top of the chart. ❜

Steve Jobs

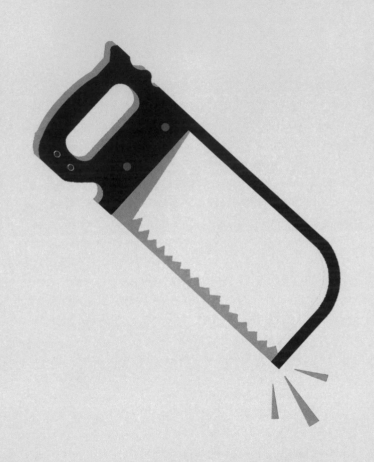

It's one thing to promise yourself you are going to change, to do more of the things you love, and say no to the things that bring no benefit or joy. You can pledge to be healthy, more attentive to the people you care about, and focus on the *one* thing that will have the biggest positive effect . . . But it's quite another thing to keep doing that tomorrow, and the day after, and the day after that. We all know change is easy to start, but harder to make stick.

Imagine trying to inflate a flat car tyre without a pump. You could try to blow the tyre up yourself, but it would be a waste of time. You would expend all your energy without result. The same is true of life. Without the right tools, we can find ourselves investing a lot of time and energy with limited results. If we really want to make changes, and get more of the stuff that makes us happy, we need to use the right tools. You can inflate a car tyre in minutes using a cheap foot pump. Simple tools can produce impressive results.

Once you know what really matters in your life – your business, your career or your health – then you can begin to focus on taking the actions that will make the biggest difference to you. Focused, decisive action makes a huge difference. Making the phone call that you've been putting off for weeks or months will make a difference. Scheduling a visit to the theatre with your best friend or booking a course you've been meaning to go on will make a difference.

These may seem like small changes, but they create a

foundation of confidence and build momentum towards achieving your true goals and dreams. By filtering out the stuff you don't want, you get more time for the things you do.

Develop the 'action habit'

I find happiness in making the most of the skills and the talents I have, and giving myself permission to dream big while appreciating everything that I already have. Action brings your body and your mind into the present moment. This awareness of what you are doing right now allows your thoughts to be focused, rather than scattered and constantly flitting between something in the future or the past, and all the things you're *not* doing. The 'action habit' is the most powerful tool I've discovered to allow me to step through my fears and take on the type of projects I might never have 'thought' feasible. Action simply makes so much more possible.

We tend to believe that we must be highly motivated before we can do or start anything. But psychologically we actually become motivated by the doing, rather than the other way round. You are far more likely to feel motivated to run after you start running than before.

When you wake up, going for a run might be the last thing you want to do, but if you create the right conditions then you'll be out the door before you know it. There have been so many times that my good intentions of early morning exercise have come to nothing. I've woken up, checked my emails and before I know it two hours have gone by. So now

I lay out my running clothes the night before; that way I can just get up, put them on and go before anything gets a chance to distract me. Simple, but it gets results.

All of the productivity 'tools' in this section will help you stop putting off what's important and get into a habit of action. When I work with clients, they often want me to just tell them how to do *more*, without first pruning and filtering so that they can concentrate on what actually matters and gets results. When you have an understanding of how you want your life to be, these are the tools that will help get you there quicker.

Ask yourself two essential questions: what is the most important thing that needs to be done today? What actions can I take or stop taking to give me the time and space to do it?

DEVELOPING THE 'ACTION HABIT'

**FIRST SET YOUR GOAL
THEN PLAN HOW TO GET THERE:**

GOAL: LOSE 14 LB IN 8 WEEKS.

STEP 1: NO BREAD WITH MEALS.

**STEP 2: PUT EXERCISE CLOTHES AT
END OF BED EVERY NIGHT.**

**STEP 3: CLEAR OUT THE 'CRAP'
FROM YOUR FOOD CUPBOARD.**

THAT'S ALL!

10. THE POWER OF SIMPLICITY

❝ Three Rules of Work: out of clutter find simplicity; from discord find harmony; in the middle of difficulty lies opportunity. ❞

Albert Einstein

It's easy to let 'stuff' mount up to such an extent that it starts to become overwhelming and makes us feel hemmed in. We simply have too much 'clutter'. Whether it's physical objects, mind clutter in the form of endless lists and things we are supposed to remember to do, or digital clutter such as inboxes with hundreds of emails, just sitting there and so many 'productivity' apps that we spend more time working out which one we are meant to be using than getting anything useful done.

I can always tell when I am trying to do too much and need to get back to focusing on what really matters by the state of my office at home. It's a physical reflection of what's going on in my head, and therefore I've made it a regular ritual to be ruthless with my space, filing anything I need to keep, clearing the surfaces of dross and creating a sense of calm and space. The concept of decluttering can seem trivial in the context of a career or a business, but it's like laying the foundations of a house: without them the house won't stand for long.

It's impossible to create your best work when your brain is cluttered. The same is true of your working environment. There is a reason why most creative people like open space: the expanse gives your mind space to think without barriers or limitations. We may not all be able to live by the beach or look out on to open fields but we can all create a better space to think, whether that's physical or digital or, ideally, both.

Think of a well-run restaurant kitchen; not only is the food delicious, cooked on time and beautifully presented, behind the scenes everything is clean, ordered and uncluttered so that the chefs can focus on the task at hand. From simplicity comes calm focus and purpose. If pots and pans were allowed to stack up, the system would begin to break down, everyone would get in the way of each other and chaos would eventually ensue.

If you've let things build up then you might not want to try to clear everything all in one go, although I'm an all-or-nothing type of person, so I find that spending an entire day clearing out my junk at home or work is the best way. I like letting rip and just getting on with the job.

You can use the concept of clearing out clutter for just about any aspect of work or life that feels overwhelming. Take your diary, for example; if it's heaving with so many meetings that you are starting to feel like you're just running from one to the next without being able to pay attention to any of them, stop and set aside a moment of calm, have a cup of coffee and take a hard look at what's coming up to see what you could either move to a less cluttered date, delegate to someone else or simply cancel.

If you only manage your diary by looking at it week to week, it will always end up overflowing with appointments. You need to look further ahead and make sure the next few months feel balanced, and that you have space left for spontaneity, opportunities and time to think and be creative.

Why we all need to declutter

Your brain is a lot like your wardrobe – stuffed with things that hardly ever see the light of day. Likewise, our busy lives are often overflowing with things we can't find or for which we can't remember their purpose, so much so that many of the good things we already possess become hidden beneath the clutter. Everyone I know owns clothes they haven't worn in over a year and probably never will again. Why do we keep them? Because we view them as an investment, so we don't want to throw them out or feel like we've wasted money buying them. But as soon as we have a clear-out and give them away we forget we ever had them. Here's a good litmus test – look at anything you haven't worn in the last three months and ask yourself, 'If I didn't own that, would I buy it?' If you even hesitate to say yes, it's time to take it to the charity shop.

Pruning leads to improving

I always find it easier to clear physical clutter before I clear mental clutter. You could start by having a weekend purge of your cupboards, make your kitchen a temple to your health, or plough through the paperwork that's been stacked up for months. Pick a room that will give you the most immediate return for your efforts. Start somewhere, anywhere. Ditching the stuff you no longer need or want may not give you that promotion you've been dreaming about but it will bring satisfaction and make you feel better equipped to tackle the bigger things you've been putting off.

Here are the rules of decluttering:

1. Use it or lose it. If you haven't worn a piece of clothing for a year, chances are you will never use it again. Same thing goes for kitchen appliances, exercise equipment, old crafts supplies, books . . . almost anything!
2. Create a 'no clutter zone' for your office space, whether that's at home or at work.
3. Buy storage boxes, a shredder and a scanner. These three things will save your sanity. It is possible to have an (almost) paperless office, but you need to shred what you don't need and scan what you do. This is where you work, where you need to create and think. Give yourself the best chance of succeeding by giving your mind the space it needs.
4. Apply point 3 at home. If you can never find your keys, buy a key rack and put it up in the hallway. As soon as you come in the door, hang your keys up. Think this is basic stuff? It might be, but how much time have you wasted looking for your keys when the solution is so simple.

A conversation I overheard on the train:

Woman A: I really need to have a clear out of the apartment.

Woman B: OK, what are you going to do?

Woman A: Well, all that stuff in the living room is ready for getting rid of.

Woman B: OK, so how are you going to get rid of it?

Woman A: Well, I was thinking that . . . oh, by the way, did you hear all that noise from the flat below last night? I almost went down there. [*Looks at iPhone*] Oh, look, here's a tip about how to get more things done. 'Try finishing what you start for a day.' Ha, ha, we were just talking about that!

Woman A never did answer that simple question, 'What are you going to do?' It was quite a masterclass in distraction.

Digital detoxing

The thought of having a digital detox used to bring me out in a cold sweat. My email inbox full to bursting, I had a reading list as long as your arm, things I needed to tweet, blog, share. How could I get rid of any of that? It's not just the amount of information we're trying to digest every day, it's the immediacy of communication – we're available 24/7 and people expect answers straight away. I know because I am guilty of this too. If I don't get a reply to my email in less than five minutes, I send out a search party.

We all need boundaries when it comes to our digital world, and we need to work these out according to what type of job we have or business we are a part of. Consistency is the key, both when using digital media to our advantage and in giving us the space we need from it. You need to create a plan that works not just for you but for the people you work with too. If everyone you work with is aware you only check emails three times a day then they also need to know you will respond to an SMS if something is urgent.

Having a digital declutter does not mean being irresponsible or being unavailable when people need you; it means streamlining how you work so you can achieve greater results for everyone.

If it's good enough for Google

In an experiment to help Google employees relax in the evenings, their Dublin office staff members were asked to drop off all their devices at the front desk when they left for the night. Staff reported 'blissful, stress-free evenings' as the company had created the conditions where everyone was expected to switch off for a few hours and be unavailable.

This reflects similar findings in a study conducted by the University of California and US Army researchers. Computer-dependent civilian employees at one of the army's stations were banned from checking email for five work days. Heart monitors were used for the week before the ban and during it to check stress levels; unsurprisingly participants were less stressed when they didn't check email. Monitors also tracked how often the employees switched from task to task during this period. During the week without email they switched half as much and managers reported more productive and higher quality work from their teams.

We can't all switch off our email for a week, but whether we switch off in the evening or create a system of checking emails a limited number of times a day, breaking free from a pattern of constant self-interruption means that we are less stressed and more productive. That must make it worth a try.

Are you on purpose or on Facebook?

The creative and early adopter side of me always wants to keep on discovering new things, but I know I can spot the signs now when I'm encountering too many shiny new distractions: blogs, websites, apps. I've been known to get my team working with a new project management tool, only to change my mind a week later. That's not productive.

Dozens of books have been written about avoiding such behaviour, but it's not always practical in the real world. The only project management tool that works is the one that works for you. The only ones I use now are Evernote and Asana (see page 220–21).

When I am in need of digital detoxing, I get started with some simple clearing by unsubscribing from all the junk mail I receive. The next step is to separate your email inbox from your task manager or your to-do list. Emails should be for communication only, i.e. if they are in your inbox then you need to reply to them now. If you need to keep them for later action, file them and schedule the action in your task manager. Anything else can be archived or deleted.

It might sound impossible, but a digital sundown is crucial, especially if you are on the computer for most of the day. Set yourself a time in the evening, ideally two hours before you go to bed, to switch off from your phone and laptop. It will help you sleep better and hopefully stop you from reaching for your phone when you wake up in the middle of the night. (I'm speaking from experience!)

During the day, try turning off all the sound alerts on your phone so it doesn't 'ping' incessantly. Check your emails in batches (yes, this works) when you can answer them with some focus instead of being constantly bombarded when you are meant to be getting on with other things.

Less is definitely more when it comes to using social media to best effect. I don't mean that you need to post only once a month, but unless you have a whole team of people dedicated to social media, then you need to work out which platforms work for you and focus on those. I get a lot of return from the time I spend on it. The core of your online marketing is your email list, not your followers. Be clear about why you're engaging with social media and if it's just to stay in touch with people, that's absolutely fine too, but don't pretend to yourself that it's for 'business'. If it is for work, then think about the quality of the content you're sharing, not just the quantity. Remember the maxim: **Less, but better.**

Being constantly available shouldn't mean you take work on holiday. Naturally, there will be times when you have no choice but to take part in a conference call or answer an important email, but that should be the exception and not the rule. (Note: I edited this book while on holiday, but when you're doing what you love and you've learned to focus all your efforts on what really matters, and are editing between cooling off in the pool, it doesn't really feel like work.) If you don't get a genuine break from work on a regular basis, you will find yourself on the road to burnout or, worse, falling out of love with your job or business. Like any good relationship, you need at least some time apart.

❛ *Let there be spaces in our togetherness.* ❜
Kahlil Gibran

Of course, we can feel comforted by the fact that our team still need us when we should be relaxing on the beach, but the biggest compliment to our leadership skills is when we have a team we can rely on. A good technique is to switch your email off when you are away and just give a few key people an emergency contact number. You might be surprised how few things really need your immediate attention.

< EXERCISE >

GET OUTSIDE

Working on a project, but hitting a wall? Lacking motivation? Losing your creative flow? Can't find a solution?

Get Outside!

Yes, it's simple, but it works. Go where you can give your brain space . . . a park, a river, a beach. Not one near your office? No problem, find a library, a church, the top floor of a skyscraper or just take a walk outside. The outdoors will change your perspective even in a concrete jungle. If you ever feel stuck, or trapped in 'busyness', running from one spinning plate to another, go outside and breathe. The less stimuli and noise you have around you, the quicker you'll find the answers.

Systems

You can turn technology to your advantage and use it to do less while achieving more. First, you need to create a system to make it easier to do less. Often creative people run from systems, fearing they're being tied down, but it's the opposite. Systems give you freedom. They stop you being repetitive and wasting time.

Once you've mastered batching your time (see Chapter 12), use technology to help you make the most of it.

Use apps like Evernote to record all your ideas so you never lose any again. Take photos in Evernote of all your receipts so you don't have to spend hours hunting for the one you need, but just can't find.

Your way to app-iness

I just counted all the apps I have on my phone – 237, but if I could only keep one, which one would I keep? Evernote. I use Evernote to systematize my life; this book was written in it, all my business receipts are scanned into it, ideas for my blogs are captured in it and all my business cards are stored in it. It is like my Willy Wonka storage box . . . everything just magically appears when I need it. I have wasted weeks of my life looking for things later because I was too busy to file them or store them at the time. This is a human trait, so my belief is that instead of trying to beat ourselves up about it, we need to find solutions that work with the way we think and live. For me, Evernote does exactly that. It simplifies everything. It creates systems and structure so that I have more freedom. Every time a bill comes through the door now, I open it and scan it straight into my Evernote scanner, then shred it . . . now I can never lose it. If I'm out at an event, I use the Evernote camera app on my phone to take pictures of the business cards I'm given so a) I don't lose them, but b) I can take personal notes about the people I've met. It can help you be more creative too. Often when I'm out, I'll see something that sparks an idea for a new blog, so I capture the inspiration in Evernote – either I take a photo in the Evernote app or I just quickly add a note in my Blog Ideas folder. It's too easy for great ideas to be lost amongst the day-to-day chores.

There is an app for everyone, although I feel like I've probably tried them all! The reality is that the only one that works is the one that you use! Most of them have free versions, so try a few and the one that you're still using at the end of the month is the one you should keep.

Haven't got time to read all the books you want? Download them on Audible instead and listen to them on the way to work. Want to keep on top of the latest trends in your industry without having to read through reams of white papers and reports? Download podcasts by thought leaders in your field instead. You can even download them and listen to them while you swim (yes, swim!).

Stop putting up with s**t

It's easy to convince yourself that putting up with something is easier than sorting it out. It isn't. I will never forget listening to speaker and personal coach Laura Berman Fortgang. She said that if we are not careful our lives become crap magnets; every little bit of junk that we don't clear out or get done will stick to us and eventually there'll be no space left for the good stuff.

It's easy to assume that only the big issues prevent us getting from where we are right now to where we want to be, but there are often lots of annoying little things that are hanging around and collectively taking up too much space in our heads. With just a small surge of concentrated effort you can clear a swathe of this clutter in one go – have an admin day and just power through dozens of those small jobs you've been putting off. You'll be amazed at the relief you feel and the space you create by clearing all your admin, arranging for people to come fix the little things in the house, having the car serviced and valeted.

Simple things, but you feel great when they are done. More importantly they free up space in your brain, which lets it get on with the more important things.

Time to let go

You're going to need to make tough decisions to get rid of everything that is holding you back. In order to get more of what you want into your life, you have to make room by getting rid of the things you don't. Letting go is hard for most of us; whether it's grief, negative beliefs, guilt or the expectations of others that keep us quietly but constantly haunted by a fear of failure.

We are all individuals, and while for some people it's possible to let go of hurt or disappointment, for others a helping hand might be needed. A coach or a mentor, especially one found through personal recommendation, can provide a helpful sounding board – because often we just need to let go of the stuff that we carry in order to lighten the load. Retreats – both business and personal – have become a popular way for people to take time out from the busyness of daily life; phones and computers are switched off and you're able to retreat and reflect. As with so many things in life, it's about finding a balance that's right for you. Often it's the serious moments that remind us how important life is, that provide our wake-up calls and force us to stop in our tracks or take a different path. But when we allow our load to get too heavy, the burden of our worries stops us from doing the things our heart wants to do and becoming our true self.

Sometimes even those closest to you can appear to undermine you just as you are about to take action. Most of the time they have your best interests at heart, but it's easy to confuse being protective with a lack of belief. Such people are often your best allies in other circumstances – your parents or your partner, perhaps. But, as Steven Pressfield says, these are the people who 'love you as you are', which is great but doesn't help much when we know we want to become *more* than we are. 'But you've got a great job,' they tell us. 'I'd love to have a life like yours.' Or they worry, 'What are you going to do about money?' These comments usually come from a well-meaning place, but they hardly encourage you to pursue your dream career.

When you know in your heart that you want to do something, you've got to go out there and find your sup-porters. If you want to start your own business, join a group of people who are doing exactly the same thing so that you can talk to each other, support each other and give each other help in whatever ways you can. If you know that you need to get off the hamster wheel and change your career, don't be put off by other people's concerns for your welfare. Instead, have confidence in yourself. You know what you need to do, and as soon as others see you are following your own path, they will either join in or drift away.

11. PERSONALIZE YOUR PRODUCTIVITY

*It's not enough to be busy, so are the ants.
The question is, what are we busy about?*

Henry David Thoreau

The conditions that make us even more productive are as individual as we are. Some of us are early risers, while others are at their most productive in the evening or during the night. Some people like to break things down and work with the detail, while others get tasks done by knowing how they all relate to the bigger picture.

If I keep my focus 80 per cent on today and 20 per cent on the future, then I'm in my productivity zone. This ratio means that I spend the majority of my day doing things that need to be done, but always with an awareness of the end goals.

By keeping the finishing line for a project in sight, I don't get caught up in just tackling what is on my urgent list – I also make sure I set aside time for the important tasks that keep me moving forward.

Understand your rhythms

I'm a morning person, so much so that I'm sceptical when someone tells me they are more productive in the evening. If I want to exercise, I know I will only do it first thing in the morning. I work in short, sharp, productive bursts. I find talking to people energizing and motivating. Other people need solitude to feel refreshed (and I'm sure that some of them really do work better in the evening). We are all different; the key is understanding what works for you and then creating that environment. If your best creative hours are between 5 and 7 a.m., then humdrum tasks such as answering emails is the last thing you should do during this time.

The same principle can be applied to your personal goals too. People who lose weight successfully, for example, aren't usually those who hand over control to a diet guru or follow the latest fad religiously for two weeks only to fall off the wagon and put it all back on again. Instead, they make lasting changes by consciously making better choices. They don't force themselves to go to the gym when they hate it; instead they find their 'Soulmate Workout' as my new hero, Chalene Johnson, describes in her book *PUSH*. (Chalene is a prime example of how fit, motivating and awesome someone over forty can be. Incredible? Possible! Look her up.)

Start to learn when and where you are most productive, and set yourself up for success by making the most of that time. Do the important things when you feel fresh and energized.

Sleep

Getting a good night's sleep is one of the best ways to help yourself get more done. Too little or too much sleep will leave you feeling tired, lacking focus and with insufficient willpower and motivation to make things happen.

Before you go to bed is the time to do less. The key piece of advice when it comes to healthy sleep is having a routine, whatever that routine is. Ironically, good sleepers don't really think about it very much, they just get into bed and go to sleep. Because they sleep well, they don't feel anxious about it, so they are naturally relaxed and ready. But when you lose the ability to just sleep, sometimes you need a bit of help to get back into a better habit.

If you're someone who can go to sleep easily but who wakes up in the early hours with your head buzzing, you need to figure out the reasons why so you can address them. For some, drinking alcohol in the evening can lead to early waking as you fall into deep sleep straight away instead of a period of REM sleep first. This means you come back into REM sleep earlier than you should and this type of sleep is easier to wake from. Or maybe your head is filled with too many thoughts that you need to work through; decluttering your mind before you go to bed by writing down what's on your mind may be your answer.

I used to have this problem, so I asked my Facebook friends for their tips. Over 200 comments later, here are some of the best:
- *Have an electronic sundown an hour before you go to bed*
- *Exercise first thing in the morning*
- *Magnesium is thought to calm, and therefore aid sleep naturally*
- *Foods containing tryptophan are calming, these include milk, lettuce and bananas*
- *Apple cider vinegar and honey in hot water*
- *Meditation*
- *Create a routine*
- *Put all your thoughts down on paper or in a mind map at the end of each day*
- *Blackout blinds*
- *You might need to go to bed earlier*
- *Fall in love*

I now have a routine before I go to bed and, while I might not adhere to it every night, I always get a much better night's sleep when I do:
- *I've stopped taking my iPad to bed to watch the latest HBO drama before I fall asleep; there was just no way my brain could switch off after being so stimulated immediately before I was supposed to sleep!*

- *I take a magnesium supplement an hour before I go to bed.*
- *I turn off all electronic devices and have gone back to an old fashioned alarm – no more emails pinging me awake at 3 a.m. Ignorance is bliss . . . if I don't know someone has emailed me, I feel no desire or need to reply; at least not until the next day.*
- *And when I'm really tired, I take a bath in magnesium salts just before I go to bed.*

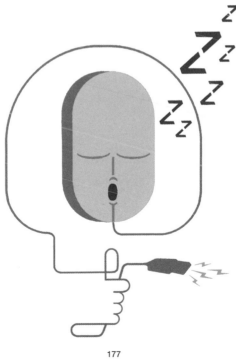

Multitasker or monotasker?

According to David Strayer, director of the applied cognition lab at the University of Utah, only 2 per cent of the population are good multitaskers, while '98 per cent of people can't multitask – they don't do either task as well'. If you are one of that 2 per cent (whom Strayer found to have brains structured differently from the 98 per cent majority), then you'll know that you can perform many tasks at the same time with no drop in performance. For everyone else, it's time to stop trying to do everything at once and focus on doing one thing at a time to ensure high levels of productivity and, ultimately, success.

Multitasking can even be dangerous; it can literally kill you. If you want to see the impact that multitasking can have on your concentration, just look at the US motor accident statistics; according to a report in *USA Today*, one in four are caused by drivers using cell phones while at the wheel.

Critical path or 'the road less travelled'

If you are already using a project/task manager like Asana, then you probably work well with system-based productivity tools. These tend to focus on 'getting things done'. You find the structure of a system helpful, and are happy to schedule your tasks and deadlines and work to a critical path. If you are naturally system-based then you will be able to tackle multiple projects as each will have its own plan and timeline.

If, like me, the words 'critical path' bring a pained expression to your face, you will naturally feel less supported by such approaches and need a clearer, simpler way to focus on the task in hand. Lots of creative people really need to put energy into 'Getting to the One Thing' (page 138); they have so many big ideas that they need to pick one and see it through before tackling the next.

Whatever your type, getting comfortable with the system-based approach is well worth while. I've benefited greatly from working through my natural resistance to adopting systems and structures. I thought they would constrain me, but in fact they've given me so much more freedom in the long run. I now see using systems as a creative tool, not a creativity killer.

Left, right or somewhere in between?

We used to think that people were either 'right brained' or 'left brained', i.e. they were either creative BIG thinkers or great 'doers' who could focus on the task in hand. You might tend towards one or the other, but essentially we all need to use both the left and right sides of our brains to succeed. We need to be able to see the big picture while also focusing on getting our next task or action completed.

Your right-side, 'get the job done' brain is great at following instructions but struggles when it comes to awareness of yourself, your dreams and what you really want out of life. Your left-side, 'original thinker' brain might have brilliant, game changing ideas but then struggles to ever make them happen. It is sensible to know on which side your own natural strengths lie, so that you can enlist the help of others whose strengths complement yours, but it's also good to know that there's nothing stopping us from being both big thinkers and doers – the key to success. Don't box yourself in.

Reboot and refresh

Exercise in the morning before your brain starts thinking about all the other things you could be doing.

To be healthy, your mind needs to do more than just think. It requires a balance of challenge, rest and different types of mental activity to stay alert, creative and productive. So, as well as getting enough restful sleep each night, you need to spend some time having fun, connecting with others, relaxing, reflecting and focusing.

We need nutritious food to feel energized and the last ingredient for healthy thinking is to add physical exercise to your day, which increases your capacity for memory and learning. After my morning run I feel as though my mind has been re-energized as well as my body. (Others say meditation does the same thing, although personally I prefer to exercise.)

Taking time for relaxation and doing less has multiple benefits. We have more time for our relationships and hobbies, we feed our soul with the space to breathe and we become more productive in a shorter time. It's difficult to appreciate this when you're feeling overworked and overstressed. Our usual response is to spend more time working when we feel under pressure, hoping that if we throw enough hours into our job then eventually we'll get on top of things.

We need to remember that, while time is finite, our energy is a renewable resource. Like a battery, even a short period spent recharging will energize us for several hours.

Simple things like going to the park at lunch time rather than eating at your desk will lead to a much more productive afternoon. Taking a holiday not only makes you more productive when you return to work but happier too. When you put off taking time off, tasks soon become boring and you drag your heels over tasks that should be quick and easy.

Your best productivity will usually come from only about four and a half hours a day – working late often means we've just been putting things off during the rest of the day and perpetuates the cycle of getting home exhausted, not having enough downtime to sleep restfully, waking up tired and repeating the pattern. Once you break the cycle and give yourself time to relax and recuperate, you're likely to find you get what used to be a whole day's work done in the first couple of hours. That means you have extra time to work on the projects that really mean something to you – and get better results.

A walk doesn't always have to be a break

Dan Pallotta, a charity activist and AIDS Ride founder, gave the closing talk at the 2013 TED Conference. It's since been viewed more than 3.4 million times and is one of the top 100 watched talks on TED.

Dan rehearsed his talk over two months during his daily three-and-a-half-mile early morning walks. He describes that after the first mile, the usual voices in his head (the doubts, the guilt trips, the fear) would quiet down and he would be left with no distractions. This was when he would get to work on his talk. Ideas would appear as if by magic, but really it was because in this space Dan was able to work at his best for this particular task. He also talks about how the people in his organization go for walks together instead of having a creative 'meeting' when they are coming up with a new campaign.

Where are you most productive?

Does your working environment hold you back? Working in an open-plan office, for example, is great for encouraging openness and teamwork in your company, but try to find an hour of quiet time and all you get is frustrated. You can't shut your door to let your colleagues know not to disturb you. You can't force yourself not to listen to the person next to you on the phone or colleagues talking about their favourite coffee hangout.

You need to tailor what you do to where you do it. If you need a quiet space every now and then, then it's up to you to create it and ask for it. This is where batching your work into different elements comes into play (page 201). Arrange a couple of mornings a week away from your desk, whether that's at home, in the library, or in a quiet corner you've managed to find.

If you are ever feeling stuck with a problem or an idea that you are working on, remember that a change of scenery can be just what your brain needs to get kick-started. If our thinking has stalled then just sitting in the same spot isn't very likely to get things moving again or going in a different direction. Take a piece of paper to the coffee shop or the park and start brainstorming. Just see what happens.

12. GET TIME ON YOUR SIDE

❛ To say 'I don't have time' is like saying
'I don't want to. ❜

Lao Tzu

We have never had so many opportunities, possibilities and ways to entertain ourselves – but are we any happier or more fulfilled than we were fifty years ago, or just a whole lot busier?

It's ironic that while so many of us feel overwhelmed by busyness, we have also become Olympic procrastinators. Our days are filled with apparently urgent demands, yet we spend ages doing nothing, trying to decide what to get on with first. Either that or we are paralysed by fears that make us nervous or worried, so that we spend all day thinking about something but never get round to doing it, and don't get much else done either in the meantime.

Time is our most valuable commodity, and yet we often waste it without thinking. That's why it's so important to give ourselves the opportunity and space to ask what really matters, what and who are important. That is where we need to focus our energies and invest our time.

Make time your ally

'I'M RUSHED OFF MY FEET'

'THERE AREN'T ENOUGH HOURS IN THE DAY'

'I'M SO BUSY'

'Not having enough time' is one of the most common excuses for not starting something or not finishing something. You can't add any more hours to the day, but you can make more efficient use of the time you have. You can certainly choose to spend your time more wisely. If you're doing what you love more often, and being with people who make you happy more often, you spend far less time caught up in anxiety and much more time getting on with things.

Be a time investor, rather than a time manager.

Value your time

If you want to use your time better – to be more fulfilled, more productive, connected – then you need to work out the value of your time and how you are spending it. For example, if you have a business, you should identify which parts of your business generate the most income or profit for you relative to the amount of time they take up. If you have a family and a career, you might work out how your time is used and realize that the time you spend cleaning would be better spent with your family, and so hire a cleaner. (Or vice versa, and hire a child minder! Just kidding, son.)

Once you place real value on your time then you can assess more effectively how you can free up more of it, in practical ways that work for you. Don't be afraid to ask yourself regularly if what you're doing right now is genuinely important or a mere distraction. This is why it's vital to align your passions and your strengths with what you do, rather than being the proverbial square peg in a round hole and constantly frustrated.

Schedule for value

We all have the same number of hours in our day, but some people learn how to use them better than others. How? It's not rocket science or magic; it's plain old scheduling. Yes, that's it. What gets scheduled, gets done.

I can guarantee that many people you admire already do this. All those people who arrive at work on Monday morning talking about their fun-packed weekends and who also hit their targets at work definitely do it. They seem to have a supernatural ability to get more hours out of each day, but it's not magic; they just waste less time and prioritize what's most important.

Learning how to schedule your life around the people and things that have true value is one of the most important changes you can make. These two fundamentally important aspects of your life, who you talk to and what you talk about, heavily influence your ability to change your circumstances and advance yourself.

< EXERCISE >

IF IT'S NOT IN THE SCHEDULE, IT WON'T HAPPEN . . .

What is the *one* thing that you used to enjoy that you really miss doing? Maybe you used to go hiking at weekends, or you used to save Sunday afternoons for reading fiction. Now take out your diary and schedule a time within the next month to do that. Don't put it off – a month is plenty of time to get something like this on the books.

➡ Who is the *one* person you love spending time with the most? Put this book down and call them, right now. Don't text, don't email, call. Right now. Ask them to get out their diary and find a time when you're both available, and don't put down the phone until you've got a date and time pinned down. Don't lose the momentum of the moment – get it scheduled!

➡ What is the *one* thing you've been meaning to do with your family, but haven't got round to? It could be going to the cinema, a day out, or just a big family meal. Whatever it is, look at your diary and schedule a time for it. Do it now. Often you probably won't even care what you end up doing, the joy is in the company.

It doesn't matter if you have to book something six months in advance. Once it is in people's diaries, or tickets have been purchased . . . it will happen. And when it does, you will ask yourself why on earth you haven't scheduled your life like this before.

Every year at least one of my holidays is with my best friend and our families. At the start of the year we decide when and where we want to go, get our diaries out and schedule it. Then we rent the villa and book the flights. No diary conflict, no urgent meeting getting in the way. It is without a doubt one of the most important things I do every year. I am always guaranteed to spend quality time with the people I love.

Study after study has shown that our greatest happiness is derived from connecting with the people we cherish. What increases that happiness even further and makes it last even longer is creating experiences and memories with those people. So why are they usually the ones relegated to the scraps of time we have left after everything else? Put the most important things and people in your life first. Don't just talk about it, do it. Commit it to writing. Schedule it.

This isn't about making your weekend look like your weekday, with every hour accounted for. This is about making sure you have time in your diary *and* your life to do the things you love, with the people you love. And making sure they don't get pushed out of the way for the humdrum monotony of everyday life.

Why not push the boat out? If you have children, you can even schedule something on a school night. It doesn't matter what it is that you want to do, but it does matter that you do it. Don't let days blur into weeks and weeks into months. Make every day count.

Scheduling is also great for giving ourselves deadlines. Knowing that we have to do something by a certain date or time heightens our focus and concentration. It's amazing how we can procrastinate for weeks or even months on end and then, as the deadline looms, act like we've just drunk ten espressos. Who knew we could get so much done in such a short space of time?

The best way to schedule for value is to create mini deadlines. When deadlines are too far in the future, they will have little impact on your sense of urgency. You can help yourself by breaking down big tasks into smaller ones that have their own (much tighter) deadlines and measurable goals. Your calendar should be your friend; schedule your tasks so that you can be as productive now as when the deadline is just days or hours away.

Time out isn't time wasted

We all think the world will end if we don't perform at a hundred miles an hour, but it won't. We've become too busy to have a life. Press pause, step off the hamster wheel, breathe and remember that life is for living.

Take a book to work, find a new coffee shop, take your lunch break at three when it's quiet, sit on your own for an hour with a cup of coffee and enjoy the simplicity of reading. You don't have to do this every day, but why not make it a weekly habit?

It is often when we are 'doing nothing' that our best ideas begin to germinate. We need relaxation to perform at our best, we feed our senses with art and culture, we remember what a big, wide world it is.

191

Have fewer meetings

Meetings: how many have you been to where you're talking about one issue, replying to an email about another under the table and still thinking of something else? Too many? Me too. The ratio of time versus value for a typical meeting is incredibly poor and yet most companies continue to put up with them; we believe if we all get into a room together on a regular basis we'll keep the wheels of productivity moving.

The reality is that too many meetings are a waste of time. We sit through an hour of people justifying why things haven't got done, or talking about things that aren't really relevant to you. We convince ourselves they are an invaluable way for everyone to catch up, and yet we already know most things on the agenda from talking to colleagues across our desks or over a cup of coffee.

Most meetings are too vague, people are allowed to waffle or go off on tangents. How many real decisions get made in meetings? They've usually been made beforehand and the subsequent meeting is there just to 'sign it off'. Even meetings intended to be a sharing of new ideas rarely live up to that billing as we usually share our ideas with colleagues beforehand so we already have a good sense of whether the idea is possible or not.

If you must have meetings, then remember 'less is more':
- *Include as few people as possible*
- *Set a clear, short agenda*
- *Set a time limit for the meeting and stick to it*
- *If there is a problem that must be solved, deal with it first*
- *Spell out the solution you decide on, and agree who is responsible for what*
- *Create a clear action plan from the meeting with a timeframe*

Focus your efforts on what you do best

Do you tend to find yourself wearing multiple hats during the day, whether because you're in charge, you're terrible at delegating, or you're a bit of a control freak? Do you hold on to tasks someone else could and really should be doing because you're worried no one else will get it right?

Trying to do everything doesn't do you or anyone else any favours, especially in the long run. You might be the 'go to' person in your business but it's difficult to stand out and be remarkable when you're trying to get ten things done at once. Plus, your work–life blend probably flew out of the window years ago and you have no idea if it will ever come back. Being that 'go to' person might be temporarily good for the ego, but it does nothing for our quality of life or the quality of our work.

Do one thing at a time – and do it really well.

When you begin your day doing that one really important thing, it's like time suddenly expands as you realize you've done the hardest task and you've still got the rest of the day. It is a tipping point of productivity – motivated by your early efficiency, you tackle the next things on your list with confidence and ease, rather than spending the whole day distracted by the anxiety of not having done that one really important thing.

Many of us have a tendency to spend a lot of our time trying to fix things that are broken, rather than doing more of what we do well. We go out searching for new customers, when our existing customers would happily buy another product from us if we just communicated with them more. We do everything except make the one phone call that could be the making of our month or year. *Today is the day to make that call.*

Becoming world class

When you focus your efforts you also begin to hone your expertise, so that rather than being a jack of all trades and master of none you increase your value in a specific area. Instead of trying to hedge your bets and have an average CV as long as your arm, isn't it better to be brilliant on one page? Becoming world class at one thing beats being 'good' at ten things. The more you can focus on your expertise, the easier it becomes to achieve more by doing less, because what you are doing is not only important to you but essential to others. It's a worthwhile exercise to take note of how focused you are on a task-by-task or day-to-day level when it comes to your strengths and expertise.

If you were to write your CV today, even if you run your own business, what would be your number one asset? What could you let go of in some areas to become world class in this specific area?

When Isaac Newton developed his *Principia Mathematica*, he shut himself off from the world almost entirely. That focus shaped scientific thinking for hundreds of years to come, and in today's age of constant interruption and multitasking, we should all learn to encourage ourselves to value quiet, focused time where we let our minds flow in and around a problem, a task or a question. That's where your genius lies. Fortunately, you don't need to put yourself into solitary confinement, but you do need to take time out on a regular basis.

When you are focused, less becomes better

A TED presentation is limited to eighteen minutes, and as Carmine Gallo writes in her book *Talk Like TED*, it doesn't matter if you're Bill Clinton or Bill Gates. 'Researchers have discovered that . . . too much information, prevents the successful transmission of ideas.' In other words, it's better to condense what you want to say into as clear and concise a message as possible, otherwise your ideas will lose their impact.

Now just because the talks are only for eighteen minutes, doesn't make it any easier. Many TED presenters will practise every day for six months before those eighteen minutes. Less time doesn't mean less effort or less impact. The eighteen-minute rule makes presenters find the shortest way to explain their idea; we could all learn a lesson from that when it comes to presenting or explaining anything that we do, make or sell. Nobody wants death by PowerPoint. Remember, a picture tells a thousand words. If our audience has to read while we're talking, what hope is there that they will really be listening. Make an impact, make an impression. Get to the point and stay on point.

It's the same process for writing – the really important part comes during the editing, when you hone your ideas and check every line, you cut out the irrelevant or the verbose so that the words you leave will speak to the reader clearly and with purpose, or at least that's what we try to do!

I'm a big-picture person, but it's good to look at the smaller picture, too. Most of the best TED talks are incredibly narrow in their focus; they give a fresh perspective on one thing. What is the most valuable idea or thing or service that you have to share? Practise it, hone it, become world class at it.

Invest in yourself

A few years ago, the ONE thing that I really wanted to do was to write a book. That was my dream, but I knew that if I was going to achieve it, I needed to focus, figure out exactly what my unique message was and how to tell it in a voice that was my own, then craft it into a book that people would relate to.

I had been wanting to write a book since I was a teenager. I just never got round to it. I created all kinds of excuses. I knew I needed some training if I was going to make it work – I'm a big believer that if you want to make something a success, you have to learn from the best, but there had always been something else I could do with my time and money. I could invest in new technology at work, a new website, a new CRM system, new offices – that was all easily justifiable, but invest in myself? Maybe next year . . .

Finally, I had one of those moments where I just thought, *If not now, then when?* This was the ONE thing I really wanted to do and wasn't doing, so I decided (against the advice of nearly all my friends, who told me I was crazy) to invest $10,000 to attend the 'Open the Kimono' (OTK) workshop in Napa, California, run by Tim Ferriss, author of *The 4-Hour Workweek*. The event was limited to 120 places and you had to apply, be interviewed and accepted in order to get a ticket. In return, Ferriss promised to share everything he knew about how to write, publish and promote a best-selling book.

I invested in the event and in myself because I knew I would gain insights I couldn't get anywhere else and I knew it would be the catalyst I needed to get on and write my own book, rather than putting it off indefinitely for the 'perfect time'. It turned out to be the best investment I made – not only did I learn from the best, but I made connections that would ultimately be life changing, including my literary agent. Yes, it cost a great deal, but focusing in on that one specific goal was so much more rewarding than trying to progress lots of different ones at the same time.

Three quick time-management tips

1. Eat that frog

Canadian entrepreneur Brian Tracy coined the brilliant phrase 'eat that frog', which is one of the best strategies for combating procrastination and getting the most challenging thing done first. We procrastinate for a number of reasons, most of which are again based in fear, whether it's fear we won't do a great job, fear we'll be rejected or fear we'll be put into the spotlight. Sometimes we procrastinate because we don't feel interested in or connected with the task at hand. That's why we need to invest a little time in looking at the bigger picture, so that we can see the steps we need to take between where we are right now and where we want to be. Remember that vulnerability is a good feeling, it's the feeling we get when we are about to grow or connect with something or someone important. And the best thing we can do when we know there's something important we are putting off is to 'eat that frog'.

At the beginning of the day, look at what you need to do and pick the thing that scares you most or that you know you've been putting off; do that first. Need to make a tricky phone call? Do that. Been putting off doing the books for months? Do it now. If you don't eat the frog, then you will spend all day worrying or being distracted by it so that you won't be able to focus on anything else. You might come up with plenty of excuses for putting it off – it's too early to phone first thing, they might be at lunch, nobody likes being interrupted in the afternoon, it's too late to call now, I'll try tomorrow – but really you are sabotaging your whole day. Then you repeat it the next day. So, eat the frog and get on with the rest of your day.

2. The Pomodoro Technique

This technique is very useful when you're starting a big, new project and you're not even sure where to begin. Buy a kitchen timer (the pomodoro version is shaped like a tomato) and before you start work set it to twenty minutes. For that twenty minutes, you do nothing except focus on the task in hand. If you have been putting off writing copy, you write for twenty minutes. If you need to mind map a new idea you have had and done nothing with, you get drawing that map. If you need to model sales projections, you do that and only that. It is a very effective way to put aside distractions and get you started. And don't worry if you don't have a tomato-shaped cooking timer, there's always an 'app for that'.

The best way for writers to overcome writer's block or for artists to find their way back to their creativity is to 'just do it'. Get up in the morning, have breakfast, and just write or draw or sculpt . . . anything. You might not always create a masterpiece, but just by going through the motions, the brain starts to kick in, catches up and things start to flow.

Tim Ferriss has one simple goal when writing:

> ❧ *My quota is two crappy pages per day. I keep it really low so I'm not so intimidated that I never get started.* ❧

It's the same for any activity or action that you know you want to do but you are struggling to get started. Don't look too far ahead, just start. If you want to go jogging but it's cold outside, start by putting on your running gear, lacing up your trainers and stepping outside. By that time, you'll just start jogging and forget what you were worrying about. If you want to cook healthier, you're not going to do it with cupboards full of junk food. Start by throwing away the crap and replace it with healthy choices.

Work or business projects can often seem too big or complicated, or reliant on external factors that prevent you from even starting. If you were to listen to every single one of your thoughts you might as well not do anything as you imagine all the ways in which taking action could lead to making a mistake and looking like a fool.

Action means putting yourself out there, at the risk of rejection; but if you try your best, then there is no such thing as personal failure. You might need to tweak your plans as you go along, you might even end up taking a radical new turn and doing something different, but it might be better.

You won't get anywhere without making a start.

Sometimes you have to simply think less and do more.

3. Batch tasks

Often the simplest things help produce the greatest results. To fast track the benefits of 'less is more', you need to nail this one thing. And it's simple.

batch: to arrange items in sets or groups

Instead of flitting from one type of task to another, batch things up to help you get more done. A typical day might include reacting to phone calls, emails or something that's 'just cropped up'. How many times have you been working on one thing, only to be distracted by another? Constantly moving from one task to another and trying to refocus your attention every time creates stress, mental fatigue, decreased creativity and a proven drop in productivity.

It's estimated that when we move from one project to another, it takes an average of fifteen minutes to regain complete focus. Not only is this mentally exhausting, but we are nowhere near as effective as we could be.

What is batching?

In its essence batching is a form of time management that allows you to leverage your powers of concentration and decrease distractions.

If you think of it in cooking terms ('How many batches of cakes are you going to make?'), it's where similar types of work are grouped together to reduce the amount of time it takes to complete the task and at the same time increase your levels of productivity and overall output.

Look at your week in advance and 'batch' time according to the nature of the tasks or projects at hand. If you do creative work as part of your day, I would advise doing it first thing in the morning before you become distracted by email, texts, Facebook or anything else. Batching works just as well at home as it does at work. For example, I find that writing of any description, whether it's my books, blogs or crafting keynote presentations, takes a different type of concentration and creativity than working through business issues.

I used to try to 'fit everything in', constantly switching from one task to the next, while checking emails, answering phone calls and trying to write a blog that I knew had to be posted the next day. That's a recipe for disaster. Setting yourself a goal of writing two blogs a week and thinking you will do it the day before it's published never works.

The best way to create great content (or anything else) is to set aside a certain amount of time each week to do JUST that. Now, instead of writing a blog because I know I 'have to get one out', I write about the topics I am passionate about and produce four in one go, but I do it all on the same day.

You can do the same with your accounts, paperwork or business planning. Set aside a defined amount of time, whether that's a day each week or three hours every Tuesday morning. Do nothing else during that time other than the tasks that are associated with that project. Be ruthless.

Getting intense

Think you have no time to exercise? Well, it's even possible to get more out of your workouts in less time, too.

High-intensity interval training (HIIT) is where you combine short intervals of high-intensity activity with slightly longer intervals of lower-intensity activity. There have been a number of studies now that show this type of exercise is much more time efficient for the results you get.

One study from McMaster University, Canada, in the Journal of Physiology, found that 'Doing 10 one-minute sprints on a standard stationary bike with about one minute of rest in between, three times a week, works as well in improving muscle as many hours of conventional long-term biking less strenuously.' You'd need to do ten hours of moderate cycling over two weeks to achieve the same fitness results. So, that's one hour of HIIT training to every ten hours of moderate training. I'll take that!

As an added bonus, the high-intensity activity stimulates your metabolism and your body continues to burn fat for twenty-four hours afterward. Less exercise, better results.

< EXERCISE >

FIVE MINUTE DAILY PLANNING

Take five minutes before your work day begins to map out your priorities.

➡️ Which frogs do I need to eat today?

➡️ What and who do I need to make time for today?

➡️ Who am I waiting for a response from?

➡️ What do I need to schedule?

➡️ What *one* thing could I do today that would take me closer to my goal?

13. DITCH IT, DO IT OR DELEGATE IT

I know that stubbornness or a 'never give up' attitude often pays off in the long run. I also know there are times when you have to recognize the difference between when you need to put in the effort to persevere because you're about to get to the good stuff and when you're putting in the effort for something that is never going to work out. You need to decide what you're going to do, delegate or ditch.

It isn't easy to know for sure when it's better to keep going and when it's better to call it a day and start something different, but there are questions you can ask yourself that will help. Don't fall into the trap of just throwing more resources at a problem until you exhaust yourself. Instead, take a moment to take stock of the situation and assess whether to continue or not. Address the heart of the matter rather than dancing around on the edges, make the tough call.

- ▶ What do your instincts tell you?
- ▶ Are you still motivated?
- ▶ Are you happy?
- ▶ Are you moving forward or treading water?
- ▶ Is your effort getting you anywhere?
- ▶ Why are you doing it?
- ▶ Is it useful?
- ▶ Are you adding value?
- ▶ Could there be an easier way?
- ▶ Could you enlist the help of others?
- ▶ If you weren't doing this, what would you be doing?

Be ruthlessly honest as you answer these questions. Sometimes, even with the best preparations and the best intentions, good ideas don't work out. It might be that you're not truly convinced yourself – if what you do isn't aligned with your purpose then it becomes something you feel obligated to do rather than something you want to do. This road only leads to frustration.

If you've fallen out of love with your business and you're carrying on solely out of duty, you need to stop. However, if you are still in love with your idea and believe in it with every bone in your body, but you're struggling to make it succeed, then you need to find the strength either to keep going or to switch tactics.

Being able to recognize the difference between what Seth Godin calls 'The Dip', which is worth working through with all your might, and a dead end is a sure-fire way to greater personal success and fulfilment. You can stop using up so much time and effort getting nowhere and have the courage to 'give up' the things that don't work in your life.

This is where we come full circle back to the U-curve of happiness. Knowing when to change course means that you no longer settle for 'tolerable mediocrity' or being good enough. In poker terms, you see good enough and raise it to being the best you can be. But to do this you need to know what you really want, because it's a fact of life that there's going to be some short-term pain before you achieve long-term gain.

Don't quit in a panic

When disaster strikes it's natural to want to either flee the scene or take cover. This is when panic sets in and you ask yourself, 'Why am I doing this?' This isn't the time to immediately give up because your good judgement may be clouded by the short-term difficulty you find yourself in. If, however, you would describe your situation as more of a general malaise where you are making a slow or no recovery, then this is the time to seriously consider a new course of action.

If you feel the onset of panic, you need to give yourself a chance to breathe and time to look at everything with a degree of perspective. Otherwise you might end up 'catastrophizing' (you miss your train and determine that your whole day is bound to be ruined) or going into 'poor me' mode, where every little thing that goes wrong is just more evidence that nothing ever seems to go right for you; you put your all into everything but never reap the rewards.

In fact, 'putting your all into everything' is the problem. Life comes down to the choices you make. We all make a few bad choices and dream the odd impossible dream, and most of us try to do too much at some time or another and end up spreading ourselves and our talents too thin. But the more we can listen carefully to what our instincts are telling us, the more we can focus on the 20 per cent of activity that brings us 80 per cent of our happiness, success, productivity – all those things – the more effectively we can decide whether to push through a difficult time or change course.

Be prepared to 'pivot'

It's essential to have a clear and simple plan because it gives you a sense of direction and it propels you forward. However, nothing in life is black and white, completely right or wrong; once you have a plan, don't hold on to it too tightly. Don't make your goal rigid – and don't be disappointed or angry if things don't turn out exactly the way you imagined they would. Sometimes a 'pivot' – a change of course to reach either the same goal or a different/more realistic one – will create a better outcome. Likewise, if you see that an old way of doing things is no longer effective, stop trying to force it to work and find a new way.

I hear so often about the 'demise of the publishing industry' or 'the end of books'. And yet I know many people who feel they are a perfect fit within the world of books; they have an absolute passion for words that tell stories, inspire and entertain. That passion isn't going to disappear any time soon, but the industry is changing. Sometimes we still want a beautiful book, or a paperback on the beach, and now increasingly we want to read on our tablet, our Kindle or our phone. If we're not browsing in bookshops so much, how can publishers let us know about books we might like to read? Word of mouth has always been the best way to sell books and it still is today – it's just that word of mouth now happens through Twitter and Facebook and LinkedIn. So a publisher's strengths and passions remain the same, and it's now a case of widening horizons and working out how to align those with the new publishing environment.

When you do less of the things that drain your energy or simply no longer work, you become open to more exciting opportunities. The important thing is to set out on your path and follow your heart. Focus on the things that you're good at and you're passionate about and strive to become world class. Then keep your eyes open to what's around you and don't become blinkered. In this way you'll be ready to spot opportunities when they arise, and you'll also be more resilient when life throws you the inevitable curve ball.

If you keep on doing what you've always done, you'll keep on getting what you've always got.

Don't be afraid to try; don't be afraid to fail.

If you don't try something you'll never know if it would have worked. Failure is not something I am afraid of any more, because I know that great things have come from the lessons I've learned along the way.

Remember that mistakes, however big, don't make you a failure. The best thing to do with mistakes is face up to them, name them and then be willing to change rather than repeat. You are not your mistakes, they are not a part of your genetic make-up. Don't let negative and limiting self-beliefs rear their ugly heads when you hit a difficult patch. It is when times get tough that we often have the biggest opportunities to learn, grow and become our true selves.

It will often be the hard thing that gets you to that place where you can do what you love and love what you do. It's the feeling that you get when you walk through the fear and make something happen, when you realize it was worth it and so much more. So long as you are committed and passionate then you never need to be afraid of either sticking or quitting. Just remember, if you can truly see a light at the end of the tunnel of resistance then keep going; if deep down you know you can't, have the courage to do something different. Even to quit, if that's what it takes.

When to do less and outsource more

You've probably already heard the story about 'Bob', the software developer who outsourced his entire job for a fifth of his six-figure salary while he surfed the web and watched cat videos. Now I'm not condoning this, but it's a really interesting, albeit extreme, example of what's possible. The thing is, his employers didn't fire him because the quality of his work had slipped, but because he was being so productive they hired a team to investigate how he was doing it. They discovered hundreds of invoices from the overseas developer Bob had hired. He was fired, of course, not least for breaching the company's security and intellectual property rights. But, on a smaller scale, this is a brilliant and a memorable lesson for us all that there are many things we could outsource, freeing up our time to do more valuable things.

When you have too much on your plate, you need to work out what really is a priority and not just a perceived one. The person who shouts the loudest is rarely the most important. Filter what you need to action, what you need to ditch and what you can delegate or outsource.

Thinking you don't have anyone to outsource or delegate

to? Think again. There are people all over the world who can help you with everything from your bookkeeping to your keynote presentation, your research, to writing or editing your blogs, to walking your dog, cleaning your home and decluttering your wardrobe. If you think doing this is a luxury you can't afford, then maybe you don't value your time enough. You can start by using Fiverr.com for, yes, as little as $5 . . . so there's no excuse.

Ditch it

You need to eliminate everything you're not going to do or delegate, otherwise you end up wasting time and money.

Ask yourself does this really need to be done? If it didn't get done, what would happen? Would it free up more time and other valuable resources if you were to stop doing it and do something else more useful?

You need to be ruthless if you want to get your life back. Often we create a rod for our own back by constantly saying yes to people which means our to-do list grows out of control. Now's the time to cut it back.

Do it

For all the actions that you absolutely have to do yourself, prioritize them, batch them and then chunk them down.

Even after you've mastered the art of 'less is more', you will still have things you need to do, but they will be the actions that will give you the greatest results.

Prioritize what is most important each day either first thing in the morning or, ideally, before you go to bed the night before, so you wake up with a clear head and a clear plan.

Now batch these priorities into the areas they fit in: work, home, personal, other . . . Tackle them one at a time, don't flit from one to the other.

Next, break up your to-do list into manageable chunks. If you're trying to do twenty things at once and think that better time management is the answer, you're wrong; what you need is *task management.*

Delegate it

If you ever find yourself struggling with something for longer than you had anticipated, it's a sign you should ask for help. Outsourcing is especially good for freelancers, consultants, small businesses with few staff and anyone working on their own projects. If you are growing a business, then knowing the ways in which you can outsource will save you significant overheads and time.

To make the most of either outsourcing or delegating you first need to sit down and work out the time-consuming, well-defined jobs that you could give to someone else. If you're a control freak then you're going to find this uncomfortable, so before you even do that try this exercise.

Think of the most successful people you know who are in your field.

Do you think they have a problem with delegating or do they turn it to their advantage?

You might want to use a mind map (page 140) here or simply note down all the things you do and put a star next to the ones that have the potential to be outsourced or delegated to another member of your team. If you are struggling at home as well as at work, then include your family in your team.

Is each of the tasks you might be able to delegate both easily defined and time-consuming for you? What would you need to do to give these tasks to someone else? For example:

- find a virtual assistant
- train a member of staff
- hire a bookkeeper or accountant
- organize an after-school rota with other parents
- hire a cleaner
- find an excellent keynote expert
- hire a gardener
- find a great graphics wizard to make your presentations fly

If you're worried that your staff or an outside company won't be able to do the task as well as you, then you need to be honest with yourself. This fear will keep you trapped. Do you want more time to spend on the really important things in your life? Do you want to do what you love, rather than carry on doing every little task because you feel so responsible for everything? If you want to change, then you need to invest the upfront time and effort it will take to instruct or train someone to do that task for you efficiently. I promise, once you get the knack of it, you'll never look back.

It might be easier to start by identifying a very specific task that would help you but you just don't have the time even to think about doing. For example, with my blog, I wanted to understand what people like to read about and engage with when it came to growing their businesses. It was impossible for me to spend days of my own time analysing other people's blogs, so I employed an online assistant to research the popular business blogs and put together an analysis of what people enjoyed or found most useful (which topics received the most feedback and engagement). As I was just starting my own blog, I didn't yet have enough followers to ask directly. But by outsourcing a time-consuming task I was able to better understand what small business owners needed and wanted and so I could focus my writing to address these questions and topics – less vague, more valuable.

< EXERCISE >

DO, DELEGATE OR DITCH

Write down your To-Do list.

Now go through your to-do list and split the tasks into the following three columns:

DELEGATE IT   **DO IT**   **DITCH IT**

CONCLUSION

WHENEVER YOU ARE FEELING OVERWHELMED, BRING A LITTLE LESS INTO YOUR LIFE

LESS PERFECTION, MORE REALITY

LESS COMPLICATION, MORE IMPACT

LESS EMBELLISHMENT, MORE PRACTICALITY

LESS IN YOUR WARDROBE, MORE IN YOUR WARDROBE YOU LOVE

LESS FOOD IN THE CUPBOARD, BETTER FOOD ON THE PLATE

LESS STRESS, MORE FUN

DON'T WASTE ANOTHER MINUTE

DON'T WASTE YOUR SKILLS OR YOUR PASSIONS

WHAT DO YOU NEED TO GET STARTED DOING WHAT MATTERS? LESS THAN YOU THINK

RESOURCES AND SOURCES

'Productivity' apps: helping you achieve more by doing less

Evernote

My everyday essential app. My digital filing cabinet in which I store all my ideas and notes. Whenever I hear anything important that I need to jot down, it goes into Evernote (otherwise I'd lose it). I can share notes with other people and all my notes sync up on all my devices (iPad, iPhone, iMac, MacBook Air).

Dropbox

Everyone in my team uses Dropbox. We can upload and share large files (presentations, videos, photos, audio files). We can share them by sending each other download links or by sharing folders. The sharing folders options mean my team can add to the folders. Super easy and efficient.

Mailbox

This handy iPhone app was recently purchased by Dropbox (it's that good). It's a quick and efficient way to manage your inbox. If you get masses of emails every day, this is the perfect app for you.

Asana mobile
A great task management app that allows you to allocate projects and tasks. The most important feature is the 'nested to-do lists' that other apps don't yet have. Worth a try.

Fiverr
A great way to outsource – everything. If you're sick of doing things that you don't like or aren't good at, or you just don't have time to do everything that needs to be done, outsource it at Fiverr.

5 Minute Journal
Leads to a happier you in five minutes. I love this app because it's a simple and effective way to reflect on my day and all the things I'm grateful for. And as you know, gratitude always leads to better things.

If you keep a short journal each day then you can monitor your progress, which motivates you to continue. You can also acknowledge setbacks and learn from them immediately, which then allows you to move on, rather than get stuck as doubts are allowed to creep back in.

Inspiring words

Shawn Achor, *The Happiness Advantage: The Seven Principles of Positive Psychology that Fuel Success and Performance at Work* (Virgin Books, 2011)

James and Claudia Altucher, *The Power of No: Because One Little Word Can Bring Health, Abundance and Happiness* (Hay House UK, 2014)

Paul Arden, *Whatever You Think, Think the Opposite* (Penguin, 2006)

Mihaly Csikszentmihalyi, *Flow: The Psychology of Happiness* (Rider, 2002)

Bill Davidow, 'Exploiting the Neuroscience of Internet Addiction', *Atlantic*, 18 July 2012, www.theatlantic.com/health/archive/2012/07/exploiting-the-neuroscience-of-internet-addiction/259820/

Timothy Ferriss, *The 4-Hour Workweek: Escape 9–5, Live Anywhere, and Join the New Rich*, expanded and updated edn (Harmony, 2009)

Tim Gill, *No Fear: Growing Up in a Risk Averse Society* (Calouste Gulbenkian Foundation, 2007); www.gulbenkian.org.uk/pdffiles/--item-1266-223-No-fear-19-12-07.pdf

Boris Groysberg and Robin Abrahams, 'Manage Your Work, Manage Your Life', *Harvard Business Review* 92(3) (2014), pp. 58–66

George Halkos and Dimitrios Bousinakis, 'The Effect of Stress and Satisfaction on Productivity', *International Journal of Productivity and Performance Management* 59(5) (2010), pp. 415–31; www.emeraldinsight.com/doi/abs/10.1108/17410401011052869

Chip and Dan Heath, *Switch: How to Change When Change Is Hard* (Random House, 2010)

Sheena S. Iyengar and Mark R. Lepper, 'When Choice is Demotivating: Can One Desire Too Much of a Good Thing?', *Journal of Personality and Social Psychology* 79(6) (2000), pp. 995–1006

Chalene Johnson, *PUSH: 30 Days to Turbocharged Habits, a Bangin' Body, and the Life You Deserve!* (Rodale, 2011)

Gabrielle Kratsas, 'Cellphone Use Causes Over 1 In 4 Car Accidents', *USA Today*, 28 March 2014, www.usatoday.com/story/money/cars/2014/03/28/cellphone-use-1-in-4-car-crashes/7018505/

Jonathan P. Little, Adeel S. Safdar, Geoffrey P. Wilkin, Mark A. Tarnopolsky and Martin J. Gibala, 'A Practical Model of Low-Volume High-Intensity Interval Training Induces Mitochondrial Biogenesis in Human Skeletal Muscle: Potential Mechanisms', *Journal of Physiology* 3 (2010), pp. 202–10

Greg McKeown, *Essentialism: The Disciplined Pursuit of Less* (Virgin Books, 2014)

Stephen Moss, 'Natural Childhood', report for the National Trust; www.nationaltrust.org.uk/document-1355766991839/

Dan Pallotta, 'The Way We Think About Charity Is Dead Wrong', TED Talk, March 2013; www.ted.com/talks/dan_pallotta_the_way_we_think_about_charity_is_dead_wrong?language=en

Kim John Payne, *Simplicity Parenting: Using the Extraordinary Power of Less to Raise Calmer, Happier, and More Secure Kids* (Ballantine Books, 2009)

Steven Pressfield, *Do the Work: Overcome Resistance and Get Out of Your Own Way* (Amazon Publishing, 2011)

Barry Schwartz, *The Paradox of Choice: Why More Is Less* (Harper Perennial, 2005)

Dan Siegel, 'The Healthy Mind Platter', www.drdansiegel.com/resources/healthy_mind_platter/

David Strayer, 'Driver Distraction and Cell Phones', www.gocognitive.net/video/david-strayer-driver-distraction-and-cell-phones

Bob Sullivan and Hugh Thompson, 'Brain, Interrupted', *The New York Times*, 3 May 2013, www.nytimes.com/2013/05/05/opinion/sunday/a-focus-on-distraction.html?_r=0

University of California at Irvine, 'Email "Vacations" Decrease Stress, Increase Concentration', news release, 3 May 2012, http://news.uci.edu/features/email-vacations-decrease-stress-increase-concentration/

ACKNOWLEDGEMENTS

'Here's to the crazy ones. The misfits. The rebels. The troublemakers. The round pegs in the square holes. The ones who see things differently . . . Because the people who are crazy enough to think they can change the world, are the ones who do' – Apple, Inc.

Thank you to all the crazy people who have believed in doing things differently.

For my incredible agent, Scott Hoffman, for being a rare combination of commercial nous and creative genius. 'Agent' doesn't even begin to credit your skills.

For Joel Rickett, my publisher, for putting his neck on the line and pushing for this relatively unknown Brit – who would have thought that little talk about social media all those years ago would have led to this (but that's for the next book!).

For the unwavering support of my friends who have supported me through everything: Lisa, Brenda, Troy, Hulya, Larry, Michelle, Chloe, Matt, Kanya, Gabby, Jamie . . . Friendship is the greatest reward.

For the inspiration to push myself to be more: Michael Fishman, Jess, Gabby, James Altucher, Christina Rasmussen, Simon, Clay Hebert, Dan and Renee, Jayson Gaignard . . . The way you guys live your lives and follow your dreams is a daily inspiration.

For Brendon for giving me the platform to realize where I really needed to be – that was a huge moment for me and I am truly grateful.

For Andrew for being the best foul-weathered friend: I adore you.

For Greg for being in my corner, holding my feet to the fire, challenging me and making me realize what I'm truly capable of. Thank you.

For my Mum and my Nan for making me believe anything and everything was possible.

Above all, this is for my spectacular son, Jett, for always shining a light on what is truly important: doing what you love, with the people you love.